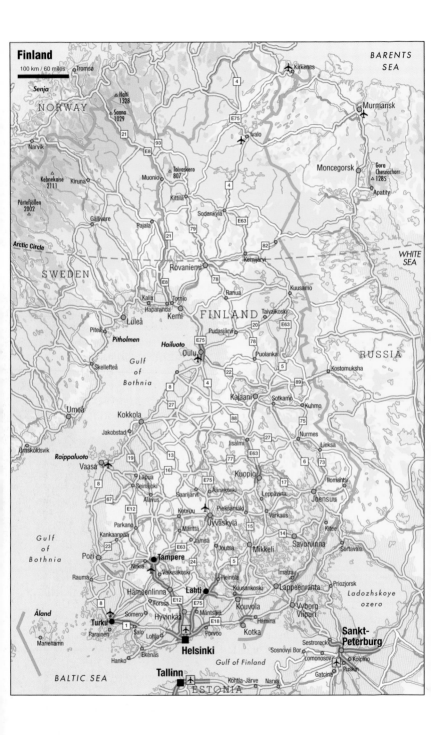

Finland

100 km / 60 miles

BARENTS SEA

Tromsø

Senja

NORWAY

Kirkenes

△ Halti 1328
△ Saana 1029

E75

Murmansk

Narvik

21

93

E8

Moncegorsk

Gora Chesnachorr △ 1285

Muonio

Toivoskero 807

Ivalo

Kebnekaise 2111
Kiruna

Kittilä

4

Apatity

Pårtefjällen 2002 △

Gällivare
Pajala

Sodankylä

E63

SWEDEN

21

79

82

Arctic Circle

Rovaniemi

Kemijärvi

WHITE SEA

E8

78

Ranua

Kuusamo

RUSSIA

Kalix
Tornio
Haparanda

Kemi

FINLAND

Taivalkoski

Luleå

Piteå

Pudasjärvi

20

E63

Pitholmen

Hailuoto

E75

78

Puolanka

Kostomuksha

Skellefteå

Oulu

22

5

8

4

89

Gulf of Bothnia

27

Kajaani

Sotkamo

Kuhmo

Umeå

Kokkola

88

75

Örnsköldsvik

Jakobstad

Iisalmi

Nurmes

Lieksa

Raippaluoto

19

13

27

6

73

Vaasa

16

77

E63

Ilomantsi

8

Lapua
Seinäjoki

Saarijärvi

Kuopio

17

67

Alavus

E75

Äänekoski

Joensuu

E12

Kuuru
Parkano

Pieksämäki

Leppävirta

Mänttä

Jyväskylä

Varkaus

Kitee

Kankaanpää

Jämsä

15

14

Savonlinna

Gulf of Bothnia

23

Pori

Joutsa

Mikkeli

Sortavala

Tampere

24

5

Ladozhskoye ozero

Rauma

Nokia
Valkeakoski

Heinola

Imatra

Priozjorsk

Hämeenlinna

Lahti

Kuusankoski

Lappeenranta

8

Forssa

E12

E75

Mäntsälä

Kouvola

Vyborg
Viipuri

Åland

Somero

Hyvinkää

E18

Hamina

Turku

1

Salo

Lohja

Porvoo

Kotka

Sankt-Peterburg

Parainen

Sestroreck

Mariehamn

Ekenäs

Helsinki

Sosnovyy Bor

Lomonosov

Kolpino
Puskin

Hanko

Gulf of Finland

Gatcina

Tallinn

Kohtla-Järve

Narva

BALTIC SEA

ESTONIA

introduction

Welcome

This is one of 133 itinerary-based *Pocket Guides* produced by the editors of Insight Guides, whose books have set the standard for visual travel guides since 1970. With top-quality photography and authoritative recommendations, this guidebook brings you the very best of Helsinki in a series of tailor-made routes devised by Insight's Finland correspondent, Norman Renouf.

This northerly capital is a vibrant, modern city, but nature is never far away – the Baltic Sea pushes its cold fingers into the city in several places, and long, dark winters prompt an enthusiastic celebration of midsummer and a host of other summer festivities, including those featuring the works of Finland's great composer, Jean Sibelius. Excellent museums illustrate an eventful past that has seen Finland pulled back and forth from West to East and back again, and magnificent churches and cathedrals are testament to the constancy of religious life during troubled times. The itineraries in this book are designed to show you the best of the city in easy stages, from the entertainment district to the cathedral, from colourful markets to first-rate museums and galleries, and from the historic Suomenlinna Fortress to dignified state architecture. Then we head out of Helsinki with three excursions to interesting nearby towns that offer a completely different perspective on Finnish history and to a fourth that crosses the border to Tallinn, the capital of Estonia, whose medieval heart is a UNESCO World Heritage Site.

Norman Renouf was born in London and educated at Charlton Central School, Greenwich. From 1962 until 1989 he worked in a variety of financial institutions in both London and the United States. Always interested in travel, he started writing travel guides, articles, and newspaper contributions in the early 1990s and has covered destinations throughout Scandinavia, Finland, Tallinn, Estonia, St Petersburg, Russia and Switzerland, as well as Spain and its islands, and Portugal and Madeira. In the Insight Pocket Guide series, he is also the editor of Insight Pocket Guide: Washington D.C

HISTORY AND CULTURE

CITY ITINERARIES

History
&Culture

The original indigenous inhabitants of the region that is today's Finland were the Sami. They were also known as Lapps, but this name is not favoured by today's Finns, who are descendants of the Fenno-Ugrian tribes that once lived in northeastern Europe between the Volga River and the Ural Mountains. They migrated north and west and, by 2000–1000BC, forms of Finnish were spoken on both sides of the Gulf of Finland. These newcomers gradually forced the Sami people out of the south and central regions to the far north, where they still live today.

The Fenno-Ugrian people were hunters and fishermen who lived in widely scattered settlements, but by 500BC agriculture had become the dominant way of life and they began to trade their fish and furs for other goods and establish a more settled way of life. We know little about their death rituals but we do know that their dead were placed in stone-covered tombs, as thousands of them have been found in the country. Later, around AD800–1050, the Vikings used what is now the southern coastline of Finland as a trade route to the east.

The Swedish Era

Until the middle of the 12th century the area now known as Finland was a political void coveted by both its western and eastern neighbours – the Roman Catholic Swedes and Greek Orthodox Novgorod (Russia). In 1155 Sweden committed to the First Crusade to Finland, led by King Erik and Bishop Henry of England – the former became Sweden's patron saint and the latter Finland's. In 1229 the bishop's seat moved to Turku, which became the capital of the eastern half of the kingdom. Around 1240 Birger Jarl initiated the Second Crusade when he led Swedish crusaders to reclaim Karelia, but he was defeated by Alexander Nevsky, who also prevented the Teutonic knights from invading from the south two years later. The Third Crusade, in 1293, established the border between the Catholic and Orthodox areas that was to stand for many centuries; Viborg/Viipuri, with its imposing castle, was founded to defend the line. However, it wasn't until 1323, and the peace treaty of Pähkinäsaari between Sweden and Novgorod, that the eastern part of Karelia became part of Russia and the eastern border was, for the first time, defined.

Soon, Swedish political and social systems began to flourish, but Finnish peasants retained their personal freedom and were never serfs. Finns were given the right to vote in the election for the king in 1362 and later for representation in the Swedish Diet (parliament). From the late 14th to the

Left: Sami life as captured by the Sami artist Alariesto
Right: Erik King of Sweden led a crusade into Finland in 1155

early 16th century Denmark, Norway and Sweden were united in the Kalmar Union. The Reformation reached Finland in 1527, when it became Lutheran. This initiated a surge of interest in the Finnish language, and the prominent proponent of the Protestant Reformation, Mikael Agricola (1510–57), Bishop of Turku and creator of written Finnish, translated the New Testament into that language in 1548.

The Founding of Helsinki

Helsinki, or Helsingfors in Swedish, was founded by King Gustav Vasa of Sweden to offer trading competition to Tallinn, the Hanseatic League city on the opposite side of the Gulf of Finland. To achieve this he issued an edict, on 12 June 1550, ordering citizens from Rauma, Ulvila, Tammisaari and Porvoo to move into the new town at the mouth of the River Vantaa. This date is now celebrated as Helsinki Day. At that time the town was very small, and became even smaller when many of its inhabitants were killed by the plague and a great fire that struck in 1570. Economic growth was slow, but continuing wars saw Helsinki become an important military centre and a winter haven for the navy. By 1640 the town had moved to its present location, further south on the Vironniemi headland. In 1654 another great fire caused devastation, only to be followed in 1710 by a further outbreak of plague that killed approximately 1,200 – around two-thirds of the population.

In 1700 the Great Northern War broke out between Sweden and Russia, and in 1703, Russia, a growing power, built a new capital at nearby St Petersburg – a move that proved influential in Helsinki's growth. However, during what was known as the 'Great Hate', from 1713–21, Russia occupied Helsinki. The Russians were driven out, but two decades later, in 1742, they returned and after this Sweden's position as a superpower began to wane. Consequently, it became necessary for Sweden to reinforce Helsinki and it did so by beginning construction, in 1748, of the sea-fortress of Sveaborg – now Suomenlinna – on a series of small islands guarding the marine approaches to the city *(see page 43)*. When completed some 40 years later, it was considered the 'Gibraltar of the North'.

This brought increased prosperity to Helsinki, and seafaring trade developed significantly, but more trouble was on the horizon. Fires destroyed Helsinki in 1808 and, in the same year, political machinations between Napoleon and Tsar Alexander I forced Sweden into the disastrous decision of declaring war on Russia. Helsinki was soon overrun. In the Peace Treaty signed on 17 September 1809 between Russia and Sweden, the latter accepted that it had lost control of Finland. Previously simply a group of provinces, Finland was then annexed to Russia as an Autonomous Grand Duchy in 1809.

Above: the founder of Helsinki, King Gustav Vasa, is crowned

history/culture

Russian Rule

The Russian Emperor Alexander I, the Grand Duke, ruled Finland through a Governor General, effectively meaning that other Russian authorities were bypassed. During his rule, from 1809–25, he governed wisely, giving Finland an extensive amount of autonomy, creating the Finnish state and retaining the Lutheran religion and Swedish as the official language. Up until this time Turku had been the capital, but this changed in 1812 when, by Imperial Edict, Helsinki was declared the capital of the Grand Duchy of Finland. In 1828 Finland's only university opened in Helsinki, having been moved from Turku after a fire.

Finnish nationalism flourished under Russian rule, with the new capital rebuilt in monumental Empire style at the hands of Carl Ludwig Engel and Johan Albrecht Ehrenström; the finest example was the cathedral, which was completed in 1852. During this period the city's population increased to around 50,000 – four decades earlier it had been just 4,000 – and daily life was very similar to that in other European cities. The Kaivopuisto Spa was extremely popular with the affluent classes, who were not allowed, by law, to travel outside the empire to seek such pleasures elsewhere. During the Crimean War (1853–56), which was fought on many fronts, Svaeborg (Suomenlinna) was still the gateway to St Petersburg and during a period of 46 hours allied warships bombarded the fortress with no fewer than 20,000 shells. The fort was forced to submit, but the city itself escaped damage.

Finnish versus Swedish

During the reign of Alexander II (1855–81) sections of the population began agitating for the Finnish language to be a joint official language with Swedish. J V Snellman (1806–81), a senator and professor at the University of Helsinki, worked hard to achieve this end. The Language Decree, issued in 1863, started a process that succeeded three years later, but even though only a small minority spoke Swedish, that language remained dominant until the early 20th century.

The city soon became Finland's administrative centre and the opening of railway lines, to Hämeenlinna in 1862 and St Petersburg in 1870, ensured that it also became the industrial heart of the country. After more than 50 years, the Finnish Diet met in 1863, and 15 years later the Conscription Act raised a Finnish army. Coinciding with this industrialisation, grand neo-Renaissance buildings – most notably along Esplanadi, Aleksanterinkatu, Mannerheimintie and Erottja – began gracing the city. Finally, after a period of more than 300 years, Helsinki achieved the primary ambition of King Gustav Vasa of Sweden, and eclipsed Tallinn as the most important city on the Gulf of Finland.

To all intents and purposes, Finland was a state within a state and was even divided from the Russian Empire by an official border. This soon caused new problems as Russian nationalism flourished during the reign of Alexander III (1881–94) and, even more so, during that of Nicolas II (1894–1917), and its adherents grew impatient with the privileges enjoyed by the autonomous Grand Duchy of Finland. Russification, the policy of overturning Finnish separatism, flourished in Russia from 1899–1917, with only a short break during the 1905 Revolution. Ironically, this was at a time when Finland was undergoing radical reform, which included moving to a unicameral parliament and, in 1906, allowing universal suffrage. Finland was the first country in Europe, and second in the world (after New Zealand), to allow women to vote and to run for parliament. In the first parliamentary session there was a total of 19 women representatives.

Independence

The arrival of the new century, along with more strident thoughts of nationalism, saw the building in Helsinki of a number of grand new buildings like the Central Railway Station, the National Museum and the Kallio Church, all in Art Nouveau style, which was also known by its German name, *Jugendstil.* The first Finnish opera was performed in 1852, and this became an established national art form. The composer Jean Sibelius (1865–1957) incorporated operatic forms in such works as the *Karelia Suite* in 1893, and his even better-known *Finlandia,* some years later, to encourage the Finnish nationalist movement and the drive for autonomy. In 1897 Sibelius was awarded an annual state grant for life so that he could concentrate on composition.

Seizing the moment as Russia underwent the October Revolution, Finland declared independence on 6 December 1917, and Helsinki became the capital of the Sovereign Republic of Finland. Yet the continued presence of Russian troops within the new country's boundaries caused turmoil that resulted in a civil war, and in January 1918 the government was forced to flee. A coalition of Finnish Socialists and the Red Guard then announced the formation of a People's Republic of Finland. It was left to the White Army, led by General Carl Gustav Emil Mannerheim (1867–1951), reinforced by forces from the Imperial German Army's Baltic Division, to regain control of Helsinki. Following German defeat and the retreat of their troops, Finland's independence was assured. After flirting with the idea of becoming a monarchy – which ended when the German Prince Friedrich Karl of Hesse refused to accept the crown – in 1919 Finland adopted a republican constitution, allowing for a strong president.

Shortly afterwards a new style of architecture surfaced, most notably in the impressive silhouette of the parliament building, which opened in 1931, and the stadium and other related arenas, built for the Olympic

Above: the Finnish composer Jean Sibelius (1865–1957)

Games of 1940. However, the games were postponed because of the outbreak of war, and the XV Olympiad was not held until the summer of 1952.

On 30 November 1939, more than a million troops from the Soviet Union attacked Finland. The resistance, led by the heavily outnumbered, ski-suited troops, repulsed the attacks and inflicted heavy losses on the Russians, but was forced to cede the southeastern part of the country to the USSR. Helsinki, however, was only bombarded a few times.

During the so-called Continuation War (1941–44) Helsinki was attacked by much heavier air raids but suffered comparatively little damage, and Finland became the only country in continental Europe involved in World War II not to be occupied by foreign forces. In 1944 the hero of the war, Marshal Mannerheim, was given his due recognition and elected president; such was his prestige that his funeral, on a bitterly cold winter day in early 1951, brought Helsinki to a standstill.

The Years of Danger

However, danger was still lurking during the period 1944–48 (actually known as the Years of Danger), when a communist takeover was considered a possibility. This threat was averted with the signing of the Treaty of Friendship, Co-operation and Mutual Assistance (known as YYA in Finland) with the Soviet Union in 1948. This guaranteed Finland's sovereignty, but committed the country to defend its borders against Germany, or any state aligned with Germany, that could use Finland to attack the Soviet Union.

The post-war years saw Finland change from a mainly agrarian country to a modern industrial one and, in consequence, the towns of southern Finland, particularly Helsinki, underwent exponential growth. In 1965, by which time it had a full metropolitan area, the combined population had grown to more than half a million inhabitants. A new, more modern, style of architecture – particularly that of Alvar Aalto – became popular, with such examples as the Finlandia Hall, dating from 1971, the Opera House, which opened in 1993, and the Kiasma Museum of Modern Art, completed in 1998.

In 1955 Finland joined the United Nations and, later, the city began to host important political conferences, including the Conference on Security and Cooperation in Europe (CSCE) in 1975. When President George Bush (senior) met Russian President Mikhail Gorbachev in Helsinki in 1990 it heralded the first US–Soviet summit.

Finland became a full member of the European Union on 1 January 1995 and the national culture was not overlooked in the rest of Europe. In 2000, to celebrate the city's 450th anniversary, Helsinki was declared one of the nine European Cities of Culture for that year.

Above: a member of the Finnish Women's Army in Helsinki in World War II

The Finnish character

In the early years of the 21st century, Helsinki has a population of around 555,000 of which 87.9 percent are Finnish speaking and 6.5 percent speak Swedish. Notwithstanding the overwhelming dominance of Finnish, the city's street signs are more often than not shown in both languages – with Swedish beneath the Finnish – and there are Swedish newspapers, radio stations and so on. On the surface, there doesn't seem to be much friction between the two linguistic groups. The Finns, in their own understated manner, are a proudly patriotic people and their blue-and-white national flag is on display everywhere.

The Finns are a quiet people, by and large, and to outsiders may seem rather introspective and far less exuberant than the Danes, for example. This is particularly reflected in young children who, more often than not, seem naturally shy. Many people have an affinity with the natural world and, since much of their country is covered by forests and lakes, Finns place a great deal of importance on spending time in the countryside – often in accommodation that is rather more basic than they are accustomed to in the cities and towns.

Saunas and Interior Design

As in other Nordic countries, where long winter days make summer sunshine all the more precious, outdoor cafés and bars are popular in the warmer months. There is an increasingly wide array of restaurants with a surprisingly large selection of ethnic cuisine – particularly Russian – and nightlife is never less than lively.

An important part of the Finnish culture throughout the year – and one that cannot be missed – is the sauna, and these are found everywhere. There are public saunas, saunas in hotels and even in some restaurants, as well as in private homes, and the natural wood-burning type are the most highly valued. Contrary to what one might expect, almost all the public saunas are segregated between the sexes and, even in private homes the sexes are often not mixed when guests visit. This is a sure sign of just how seriously the Finns take this element of their culture. Historically, the sauna was the place where women gave birth and where bodies were laid out after death and, as a consequence, for most Finnish people the sauna is an experience not to be taken lightly.

The Finns' famous flair for modernist design, whose clean, functional lines have influenced ar chitecture and furniture throughout the world, is matched by their fascination for technology. As befits the home of

Nokia, almost everyone you see is carrying a mobile phone. Finland also has one of the highest ratios of people connected to the Internet, but for the visitor this actually has a downside as, unlike in many European countries, it means that Internet cafés are few and far between.

Left: Finnish design is famous throughout the world

HISTORY HIGHLIGHTS

500BC Agriculture is established as the dominant way of life for most of the inhabitants of the area.

1155 Sweden, led by King Erik and Bishop Henry of England, takes the First Crusade to Finland.

1229 The Bishop's seat moved to Turku, which becomes capital of the eastern part of the country.

circa 1240 Birger Jarl leads the Second Crusade to reclaim the eastern part of the country, Karelia, but is defeated by Alexander Nevsky.

1293 The Third Crusade establishes the border, at Viborg/Viipuri, between Sweden and Russia.

1350 Swedish National Law established in Finland.

1527 The Reformation reaches Sweden, which becomes Lutheran.

16th century Mikael Agricola, the Bishop of Turku, creates written Finnish and translates the New Testament into that language.

12 June 1550 King Gustav Vasa of Sweden founds Helsinki.

1640 Helsinki moves further south to its present location on the Vironniemi headland.

1713–21 and 1742 Russia occupies Helsinki, beginning the decline of Sweden's position as a superpower.

1748 Construction of the Suomenlinna fortress begins.

1808 Sweden declares war on Russia and is defeated.

1809 Finland, previously a group of provinces, is annexed to Russia as an Autonomous Grand Duchy.

1812 By Imperial Edict, the capital moves from Turku to Helsinki.

1812–1850s Helsinki is rebuilt in monumental Empire style.

1863 The Language Decree, activated in 1866, makes Finnish the joint official language with Swedish.

1890s Jean Sibelius, a fervent nationalist, composes the *Karelia Suite* and *Finlandia*.

1906 Finland introduces universal suffrage. It is the first country in Europe, and second in the world, to grant women the vote.

6 December 1917 During the Russian October Revolution Finland declares independence, but this is followed immediately by a short civil war.

1919 Finland adopts a republican constitution, allowing for a strong president.

1930s A new style of Functionalist architecture develops, prime examples being the Lasi Palatsi (Glass Palace) and the Olympic Stadium.

30 November 1939 The Soviet Union attacks Finland which, despite its vastly inferior number of troops, it manages to repulse.

1941–44 Helsinki is again attacked by the Soviet Union, but suffers little damage. Finland is not occupied by foreign troops.

post-war years Finland evolves from a mainly agrarian country to a mainly industrial one.

1952 Helsinki hosts the XV Olympic Games, originally scheduled for 1940 but postponed because of war.

1955 Finland joins United Nations.

1970s onwards Alvar Aalto initiates a modern style of architecture, with buildings such as the Finlandia Hall.

1 January 1995 Finland becomes a full member of the European Union.

2000 On the 450th anniversary of the city, Helsinki becomes one of nine European Cities of Culture.

2002 Euro replaces the Finnish mark.

2003 After elections, the Centre Party, Social Democratic Party and Swedish People's Party govern as a coalition.

2007 General election in March.

history/culture

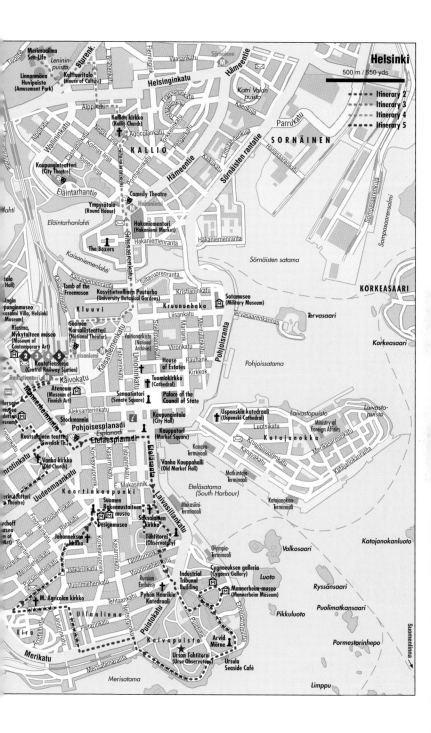

Helsinki

500 m / 550 yds

- ···■■··· Itinerary 2
- ···■■··· Itinerary 3
- ···■■··· Itinerary 4
- ···■■··· Itinerary 5

Merimaailma Sea-Life
Leninin-puisto
Linnanmäen Huvipuisto (Amusement Park)
Kulttuuritalo (House of Culture)
Sturenk.
Braheenkatu
Flemingink.
Vaasankatu
Sörnäinen
Hämeentie
Katri Valan puisto
Käenkuja

Alppikatu
Helsinginkatu
Franzeninkatu
Castreninkatu
Viipurinkatu
Porthaninkatu
Aleksis Kivenkatu
Pengerkatu
Tiilimäenkuja
Sörnäisten rantatie
Parrukatu
SÖRNÄINEN
Hanasaarenkatu

Kallion kirkko (Kallio Church)
Agricolankatu
Kaarlenkatu
Kolmas Linja
Hämeentie
Hanasaarenranta

KALLIO
Neljäs Linja
Siltasaarenkatu
Toinen Linja
Kaupunginteatteri (City Theatre)
Eläintarhantie
Sompasaarensalmi
Sompasaarenkuja
Sörnäisten rantatie

Ympyrätalo (Round House)
Comedy Theatre
Hakaniemi
Eläintarhanlahti
The Boxers
Hakaniementori (Hakaniemi Market)
Hakaniemenranta
Hakaniemenranta
Sörnäisten satama

lahti
Kaisaniemenlahti
Sillanvuorenranta

talo (Hall)
Tomb of the Freemason
Kaisaniemenranta
Kristianinkatu
KORKEASAARI

ngin punginmuseo asalmi Villa, Helsinki Museum)
Kasvitieteellinen Puutarha (University Botanical Gardens)
Liisankatu
Sotamuseo (Military Museum)
Tervasaarenkannas
Tervasaari

Kiasma, Nykytaiteen museo (Museum of Contemporary Art)
Kluuvi
Suomen Kansallisteatteri (National Theater)
KRUUNUNHAKA
Maneesik.
Mariank.
Korkeasaari

Valtionarkisto (National Archives)
Vironkatu
Pohjoisranta

Kaisaniemi
Rautatieasema (Central Railway Station)
House of Estates
Rauhank.
Kirkkok.
Pohjoissatama

Rautatientori
Kaivokatu
Ateneum (Museum of Finnish Art)
Uudenkatu
Tuomiokirkko (Cathedral)
Laivastopuisto
Laivasto-puisto

hersen museo dersen museum
Mannerheimintie
Senaatintori (Senate Square)
Palace of the Council of State
Uspenskin katedraali (Uspenski Cathedral)
Luotsikatu
Ministry of Foreign Affairs
Katajanokka

Stockmannin
Aleksanterinkatu
Kaupungintalo (City Hall)
Kruunuvuorenkatu
Kanavakatu
Meritullinkatu
Katajanokanranta

Ruotsalainen teatteri (Swedish Th.)
Pohjoisesplanadi
Esplanadi
Kauppatori (Market Square)
Kanava-Terminaali

rontinkatu
Vanha kirkko (Old Church)
Eteläesplanadi
Korkeavuorenk.
Kasarmik.
Fabianinkatu
Unioninkatu
Kauppatori
Vanha Kauppahalli (Old Market Hall)
Matkustaja-Terminaali

erin teatteri Theatre)
Kaartinkaupunki
E. Makasiink.
Eteläsatama (South Harbour)
Makasiini-Terminaali

Roobertinkatu
Suomen Rakennustaiteen museo
Designmuseo
Laivasillankatu
Olympia-Terminaali
Valkosaari
Katajanokan-Terminaali
Katajanokanluoto

ychoff useo Art)
Johanneksen kirkko
Fredrikinkatu
Iso Robertink.
Korkeavuorenk.
Kasarmik.
Suolainen kirkko
Tähtitorni (Observatory)
Olympia-Terminaali
Luoto
Ryssänsaari

Merimiehenk.
Pursimiehenkatu
Jaakarinkatu
Vuorimiehenk.
Cygnaeuksen galleria (Cygaeus' Gallery)
Mannerheim-museo (Mannerheim Museum)
Puolimatkansaari

M. Agricolan kirkko
Tehtaankatu
Russian Embassy
Pyhän Henrikin Katedraali
Industrial Tribunal Building
Pikkuluoto

Eira
Ullanlinna
Puistokatu
Pietarinkatu
Ehrenströminite
Pormestarinhepo
Suomenlinna

Merikatu
Kaptenink.
Laivurink.
Kaivopuisto
Arvid Mörne
Ursin Tähtitorni (Ursa Observatory)
Ursula Seaside Café

Merisatamanranta
Merisatama
Limppu

orientation

Orientation

Helsinki is on an oddly shaped peninsula, as the surrounding waters have found ways of cutting bays into the land. Initially, this can make this city surprisingly confusing for such a small capital, but most of the attractions are located in the city centre, which makes orientation easier for visitors. Before striking out independently, it can be well worth taking the **Audio City Tour** *(see page 86 for details)*, which gives a good overview of the city's main sites.

The core of the city is Central Railway Station, which sits in the northwest corner of a rectangular area between the Esplanadi in the south, Mannerheimintie to the east, and the Senate Square and Market Hall to the southeast. It is within this rectangle that the majority of Helsinki's hotels, shops, bars and nightclubs are to be found.

Most of the city's places of interest can be reached quite comfortably on foot, but if you do get footsore or short of time, there's a good public transport network. This includes a metro (subway) system, although most visitors prefer to remain above ground and use the tram or bus systems, which all coverge at Central Railway Station.

It doesn't make sense to rent a car here. Even the three out-of-town destinations can be easily reached by public transport, with frequent train services to Tampere and Turku, and Porvoo just a short bus trip away. Tallinn, in Estonia, on the south side of the Bay of Finland, is reached by high-speed ferry or helicopter.

The Tours

The first four itineraries in the book are full-day tours designed in half-day segments, with details of a convenient place to stop for lunch, but the sites can actually be visited in any order.

The out-of-town trips to Porvoo, Tampere and Turku – all in southern Finland – and Tallinn, in Estonia, a short hop across the bay, are intended as full-day tours, but some consideration should be given to how much time you wish to spend in each place. Porvoo is the closest, less than an hour away by bus, and could be seen in less than a full day. Trains to and from Turku and Tampere take just under two hours, and it is possible to see the most important places of interest in these towns by making an early start and a fairly late return.

The high-speed ferry to Tallinn takes just 1½ hours, but you have to be at the terminal some time before sailing and there may be a long wait to get through passport control at Tallinn. Since Tallinn has numerous attractions, it is worth considering making a two-day trip to do them justice.

Left: Upensky Cathedral
Right: soaking up the summer sunshine

1. MARKET AND SENATE SQUARES *(see map, p24)*

Visit the Market Square and South Harbour before heading for the Uspenski Orthodox Cathedral. After lunch, a short walk brings you to the majestic Senate Square (Senaatintori), with its magnificent cathedral and elegant administrative buildings.

Don't choose a Sunday for this tour – there's no market that day and cathedral opening hours are restricted. Note that our recommendation for lunch closes at 2pm.

Market Square (Kauppatori) is one of Helsinki's real delights. The market (Mon–Fri 6.30am–6pm, Sat 6.30am–4pm; from May also operates Sun 9am–5pm), in operation since the 18th century, features lots of fresh fish, especially salmon in many guises, some sold directly from small boats, and there's fruit and vegetables, numerous handicraft stalls offering souvenirs and furs, and a motley collection of outdoor cafés housed in tents. The square is also the venue for the Baltic Herring Market, held each October. The obelisk with a strange, golden, two-headed eagle is the Empress' Stone. Erected in 1835, it became Helsinki's first public memorial, commemorating Empress Alexandra's first visit to the city two years earlier. However, the eagle was removed by Russian sailors in 1917, during the Revolution, and wasn't replaced until 1972.

In the **South Harbour**, there are massive Silja, Viking Line and other ferries that, in the winter months, need to have a way cleared for them through the ice that covers the water. The sea begins to freeze soon after Christmas and can reach a thickness of 50cm (20ins). The city keeps nine impressive icebreakers on hand to clear all the necessary channels. Ferry boats to Suomenlinna also start from here, as do other cruises.

Of real interest is the red, white and yellow brick **Old Market Hall** (www.wanhakauppahalli.com; Mon–Fri 8am–6pm, Sat 8am–4pm) just a few metres around the harbour, which was the first of its kind in Finland when it opened in 1889. There is a fascinating array of stalls selling delicatessen-style foods, includ-

Above: a floating vegetable stall
Left: Southern Harbour

ing such things as bear meat, bakery products and all kinds of other goodies – there's even a sushi bar.

Two other buildings come into view. The largest is the long, low, bluish-grey façade of the **City Hall** (Pohjoisesplanadi 11–13), with the city's coat-of-arms depicted on the tympanum. It dates from 1896 but was first used in its present form in 1931. On the corner sits the **Presidential Palace**, constructed in 1820 as the home of J H Heidenstrauch, a merchant and shipowner, but was soon purchased to be the residence of the Russian tzar on his visits to Finland. After Finland gained independence the building became the official residence of the president (in 1921), until a more modern residence was chosen at Mäntyniemi in the Meilahti district, near Seurasaari. These days, the palace is used for presidential functions, particularly the prestigious reception held each year on 6 December, Independence Day. Just across from it is the Main Guard Post, completed in 1843, but much modified at a later date.

Uspenski Cathedral and the Katajanokka District

The sight that will really captivate the imagination, however, is that of the 13 golden onion domes of the **Uspenski Cathedral** (tel: 634 267; Oct–Apr Tues–Fri 9.30am–4pm, Sat 9.30am–3pm, Sun 12–3pm; May–Sept Mon–Fri 9.30am–4pm, Sat 9.30am–4pm, Sun 12–3pm; closed Orthodox feast days; free) at Kanavakatu 1, on the hill at the end of the Market Square. After the Russians defeated the Swedes in 1809 they decided that a major Orthodox cathedral was needed in Helsinki. The result was this massive church, designed by Aleksi Gornostajev in the Russian Byzantine style and built on a site previously reserved for an Imperial Palace. Consecrated on 13 October 1868, it is the largest Orthodox cathedral in the Western world. When Finland gained independence, ties with the Russian Church were cut and a 1918 decree put Orthodoxy on a par with Lutheranism as the second national religion. The number of

domes on the cathedral was fixed at 13 to represent Christ and the 12 Apostles. Inside, four huge columns with paintings on their upper corners support an immense pale blue dome decorated with numerous golden stars. As is usual in Orthodox churches, there are no seats for the congregation, and many icons adorn the walls.

The cathedral is located just inside the **Katajanokka** district, which is very much a mixed bag as far as attractions are concerned. However, a short excursion is in order, from the cathedral left along Rahapajankatu, passing the Belvedere Russian restaurant, to Luotsikatu, arguably Helsinki's best-preserved street of Art Nouveau (*Jugendstil*) houses. Here, all the buildings have architectural eccentricities on display, competing with each other for attention. Note the plaque on the wall of No 5 depicting a delivery man and a horse and

cart; this commemorates the first cooperatively owned bread shop, Elanto, which opened in 1907.

Other attractions in Katajanokka are the ice–breakers moored on the northern side, and the impressive ministry of foreign affairs, which was originally designed as naval barracks in the 1820s. However, most people will be happy to return to the Market Square for lunch, where the **Café Eteläranta** (kitchen closes 2pm) is a good bet. It has a terrace overlooking the South Harbour and offers a simple, inexpensive, three-course meal – salad, main course and coffee or dessert – or you can have soup and a selection from the buffet.

City Museum

From the Market Square, go up cobbled Sofiankatu to the **Helsinki City Museum** (Helsingin kaupunginmuseo; tel: 169 3933; Mon–Fri 9am–5pm, Sat–Sun 11am–5pm; admission charge, but free on Thur) at Sofiankatu 4. The interesting exhibition entitled 'Helsinki on the Horizon' details the best and worst of the city's history. Close by, the impressive cathedral (*see page 26*) looms large at the top of a two-tiered bank of 47 stone steps, behind Senate Square.

Until 1809, Stockholm was the capital of Finland and Turku (*Åbo* in Swedish) was the administrative and spiritual centre of the country. How-

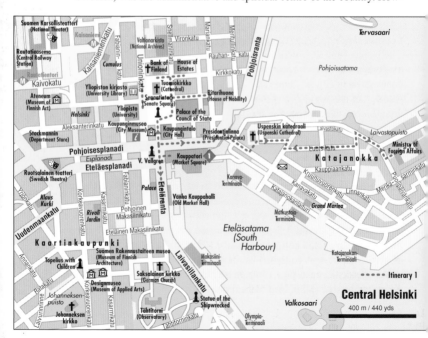

Central Helsinki

400 m / 440 yds

city itineraries

ever, things changed after Tzar Alexander of Russia proclaimed himself the constitutional ruler of the new Grand Duchy of Finland in the same year and declared Helsinki the new capital in 1812. Naturally, he wanted the capital to reflect his grandeur, so he chose Johan Albrecht Ehrenström, a military engineer and former courtier of Sweden's King Gustavus III, to lead the newly formed reconstruction committee that would transform the city in a sumptuously grand style. By 1817 his monumental town plan had been finalised. It was based around the **Senate Square** (Senaatintori) where there would be a church surrounded by administrative buildings. This was to become the symbolic heart of the new Grand Duchy of Finland where all the main institutions had an exact place according to their function in the hierarchy.

Ehrenström then selected the Prussian Carl Ludvig Engel (1778–1840) to design and oversee the whole project. Engel, who had received his architecture diploma from the Berlin Nauakademie in 1804, became city architect of Tallinn and met Ehrenström when he was working in Turku in 1814. He had spent two years in St Petersburg before Ehrenström appointed him architect of the reconstruction committee for Helsinki in 1816. His work, spanning about a quarter of a century, resulted in some 30 public structures, all in neoclassical (Empire) style, of which the most important, around Senate Square, have been preserved.

State Buildings and the University

The first building to be constructed was the main (west) wing of the Senate on the east side of the square (to the right as you face the cathedral), which opened in 1822 and was followed by the south and east wings in 1824 and 1828, respectively. It is in the shape of a large rectangle 110m (360ft) by 83m (272ft), and the pastel-coloured main wing facing the square has a domed central extension with columns and porticoes reflecting those of the Senate in Rome. After Finland gained its independence from Russia in 1917 the Economic Division of the Senate became the Government of Finland in November 1918, and the building became known as the **Palace of the Council of State**. Refurbished between 1974 and 1997, it now houses the prime minister's office, the office of the chancellor of justice, much

of the ministry of finance, and the government's conference rooms. Every Thursday at 1pm the cabinet meets in a third-floor room, and the next day at 11am they meet the president in the Throne Room, one of Finland's most beautiful Empire-style halls, to present laws that require ratification. On the palace façade the handiwork of the master clockmaker Jaako Juhonpoika Könni can be seen, in the form of the country's oldest public clock.

Left: the Alexander monument on Senate Square
Right: clouds over Senate Square

The Turku Academy, the country's first university, was founded in Turku in 1640 but in 1828, after a devastating fire, it was moved to Helsinki and placed in a prestigious location on the west side of the Senate Square. It was renamed the Tzar Alexander University, and the main building was completed in 1932. Although there are clear similarities with its neighbour across the square, Engel gave it an independent identity; in 1919 it was again renamed, to become the **University of Helsinki**.

Although not on the square itself, the pastel-yellow Empire-style **University Library** (tel: 191 23196; www.lib.helsinki.fi; Mon–Fri 9am–8pm, Sat

9am–4pm; free), next to the university building, has been praised as Engel's masterpiece and is considered a Finnish architectural landmark. Unfortunately, Engel didn't live long enough to witness its opening in 1840. Take a few minutes to view the marvellously ornate Cupola Hall, designed to resemble Roman baths. The upper area is supported by 28 marble columns, their pinnacles gilded with gold leaf, with the images and ornaments on the domed ceiling symbolising knowledge and learning. It is considered one of the world's most beautiful library buildings.

In the centre of the square is a statue of Tzar Alexander II of Russia, the most popular of the five Russian tzars who ruled Finland for 110 years, an enlightened leader whose many reforms assisted the Finns both economically and socially. Dating from 1894, it is surrounded by images representing Law *(Lex)*, Peace *(Pax)*, Light *(Lux)* and Work *(Labour)*. This square is an extremely popular meeting place for the Finnish people, and never more so than on Independence Day, 6 December, and New Year's Eve, when huge, excited crowds gather here.

Behind the square, on Aleksanterinkatu 16–18, and recognisable by its blue façade and white columns, is **Sederholm House** (Sederholmin Talo; tel: 169 3625), which dates from 1757 and is the oldest stone building in Helsinki. It is now a branch of the Helsinki City Museum.

Helsinki Cathedral

Notwithstanding all these impressive structures, it is a massive columned façade, topped by a huge dome, that dominates Senate Square, as it must have dominated Engel's thoughts when he worked on the plans from 1818 until his death in 1840. At Unioninkatu 29, Engel laid the cornerstone of the Lutheran **Helsinki Cathedral** (Tuomiokirkko; tel: 2340 6120; daily 9am–6pm; until midnight in summer; free) on 25 June 1830, the 300th anniversary of the Augsburg Confession, but it was not until 15 February 1852 that it was consecrated. It replaced an earlier church dating from 1727 and was originally known as the Church of St Nicholas – after both the

Above: the interior of the University Library
Right: the House of Nobility

city itineraries

patron saint of trade and seafaring, and Tzar Nicholas. Later, in 1959, when Helsinki became a diocesan seat, it was upgraded to the status of cathedral.

The building is in the shape of a Greek cruciform and the statues of the Apostles on the roof are the largest set of zinc sculptures in the world. The figures of angels beside the altarpiece, which was painted in the 1880s, were designed by Engel himself. Although it is sparsely decorated, the cathedral also has statues of the Reformation leaders Luther, Melanchton and Mikael Agricola. The cathedral can seat a congregation of 1,300, and the vaulted crypt is used as a venue for exhibitions and concerts. Engel also designed the two chapels on either side of the steep steps; the one to the east is still used as a chapel, and the bells and a café are contained in the western one.

The Four Estates

There are other notable buildings nearby. Sitting beside a little park is the **House of Nobility** (Ritarihuone), a brick building with Gothic influences that dates from 1862. Before the present parliamentary system came into being, the country was governed by a Four-Estate Diet, and this house was built as a meeting place for the Noble Estate. Members of the Finnish aristocracy still occupy it today. From 1863, the other three Estates – the Clergy, Burghers and Peasants – shared the house, until they moved to their own premises in 1890 *(see below)*. The walls of the banqueting hall are covered with the coats-of-arms of 358 noble Finnish families, of which some 150 still have living descendants.

Behind the cathedral, in Snellman Square, are two more impressive buildings. Following the economic expansion of the latter part of the 19th century, it was thought appropriate that the **Bank of Finland** should occupy grand premises, so this one, in the style of a Renaissance palace, was built for it in 1876–83. Outside the bank, atop a plinth, sits a statue of J V Snellman (1806–81), a statesman and leading philosopher of his day. Opposite the bank building and displaying more of an architectural flourish, is the **House of Estates**, which was built in 1890 as a meeting place for the three non-noble Estates, and they occupied it until 1906. Look, especially, for the frieze on the tympanum; it depicts Emperor Alexander I surrounded by the heads of the Four Estates and the symbols of faith and justice.

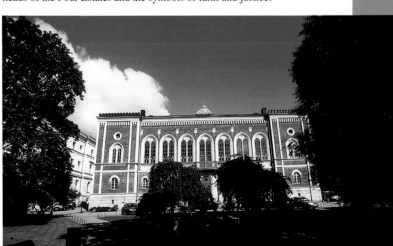

2. RAUTATIENTORI AND KAIVOPUISTO PARK *(see map, p18–19)*

Investigate the buildings around the station square before walking down Mannerheimintie, Helsinki's busiest street, then along Esplanadi. After lunch go through the delightful Kaivopuisto Park and the embassy area to the waterside and follow that to an impressive Art Nouveau district; then take a look at two impressive churches and a couple of museums.

Start at the Central Station. If you want to visit the Mannerheim Museum, note that it's not open Monday to Thursday.

Central Railway Station is one of the city's best-known historical buildings. Dominated by a massive, four-sided clock tower, it dates from the late 1910s. More than 200,000 people pass through it each day – but only half as passengers. **Railway Station Square** (Rautatientori), to the east, serves as an open-air bus station and has, on its north side, the National-Romantic style Finnish National Theatre, which has been the theatrical company's home since 1902. Outside, stands an oversized statue of playwright and novelist Alexis Kivi (1834–72). He is now recognised as one of Finland's greatest writers, although he died in obscurity.

Ateneum and Mannerheimintie

On the south side of Rautatientori, at Kaivokatu 2, is the neo-classical façade of the **Museum of Finnish Art** (Ateneum, Suomen taiteen museo; tel: 1733 6401; www.ateneum.fi; Tues and Fri 9am–6pm, Wed–Thur 9am–8pm, Sat–Sun 11am–5pm; admission charge). Inaugurated in 1887, it represented a huge investment for a small country, and its collection of more than 4,300 paintings and 750 sculptures is the largest in Finland. The works of Finnish artists date from the 1750s to the early 1960s (works from 1960 onwards are on display at the Kiasma, Museum of Contemporary Art, *see page 33*). There's also a small selection of international art (Van Gogh, Gaugin, Cézanne and Chagall), from the late 19th century to the 1950s. Next door is a 1960s shopping centre, known as the Sausage Block because of the sausage-shaped bands of concrete encircling its façade.

Just past the Cumulus Seurahuone Hotel is **Mannerheimintie**, Helsinki's busiest street, named after the respected Marshal of Finland in honour of his 75th birthday in 1942. Baron Carl Gustav Emil Mannerheim (1867–1951) was a political and military leader, explorer, general in the Russian Imperial Army and President of Finland from 1944–46, and perhaps the most influential figure in Finnish history from the Civil War to the late 1940s. At the junction with Aleksanterinkatu – a busy shopping street leading to Senate Square – Three Blacksmiths Square is named after a statue dating from 1932. Here, Mannerheimintie is dominated by the Stockmann's department store *(see page 69)*. The Stocka clock is a popular meeting place.

Above: statue of the playwright and novelist Alexis Kivi on Railway Station Square

The Esplanadi

Further along, the silhouette of the Swedish Theatre dominates the scene. In 1827 a wooden theatre designed by C L Engel was opened on the site, but the present one dates from 1866. Behind the theatre is Helsinki's most emblematic park, the **Esplanadi**. Two streets – Pohjoisesplanadi and Eteläesplanadi: North and South Esplanades, respectively – run either side of the Esplanadi, and are quite different in character. Pohjoisesplanadi is home to small shops, bars and restaurants, including the ever-popular Esplanade Café, the Kämp Hotel, and the tourist office (No 19); while Eteläesplanadi has larger institutions. These neo-Renaissance structures replaced older wooden buildings in the second half of the 19th century. Esplanadi itself is a delightful central park that runs all the way down to Market Square. The statue in the middle of the park honours J L Runeberg (1804–77), the national poet who lived in Porvoo *(see page 50)* and wrote the lyrics for the Finnish national anthem. There are two other statues of eminent men at the western end of the park, just outside the ultramodern Teatteri restaurant, bar and deli complex. One commemorates the writer, Zacharias Topelius (1818–98), the other the poet, Eino Leino

(1878–1926). At the other end, by Market Square, there is a small stage and, past that, the famous fountain featuring the naked mermaid *Havis Amanda* – erected in 1908 amid great controversy.

For lunch, you could try one of the little tent-cafés around the square. Alternatively, you could buy smoked-fish delicacies from the stalls lining the market and sit on one of the benches to eat them.

Above: *Havis Amanda*
Left: in the Esplanadi

Kaivopuisto Park

Walk back along Market Square, but turn left and, after the Old Market Hall and the Palace Hotel, follow Eteläranta and Bernhardinkatu to the red-brick, neo-Gothic **German Church** (Saksalainen kirkko; Bernhardinkatu 4; tel: 6869 8510), which was completed in 1864. Rectangular in shape, its tower was added during a 1897 reconstruction.

Move on to **Observatory Hill** (Tähtitorninmäki), which is almost directly behind the German Church and named after the **Observatory** (Tähtitorni),

which was built in 1833, designed, like so much else in the city, by C L Engel. At the centre of an attractive park, its elevated position allows for panoramic views over the South Harbour. Nearby is Robert Stigell's bronze memorial, the *Statue of the Shipwrecked,* a well-known landmark dating from 1897.

Now walk towards a row of elegant townhouses and pass a small rocky pond and fountain before walking down a ramp and some steps between the houses towards some eclectic buildings. Those to the left, shaped like a piece of cheese, are stylish, but standing behind large railings to the right is the more formidable Russian Embassy complex.

The **Cathedral of St Henry** (Pyhän Henrikin Katedraali; Puistokatu 1; tel: 637 853), built in neo-Gothic style, was opened in 1860 as a garrison church but was restyled as a cathedral when Finland received its first Catholic Bishop (there are now nearly 8,000 Roman Catholics in Finland). Statues of saints Henry, Peter and Paul adorn the cathedral façade.

To the left, the impressive, marble Industrial Tribunal building, originally built in 1916 as a private residence before becoming the Helsinki Court of Appeal, now belongs to the State. This leads to the entrance to **Kaivopuisto Park**, one of the finest in Helsinki. It was wasteland until the

1830s, a time when Helsinki was developing into a cosmopolitan spa town and was popular with Russian high society, as they were forbidden to travel outside the empire. To facilitate their visits, a regular steamer service was initiated between Helsinki, St Petersburg and Tallinn. This ritzy era didn't last long; the Crimean War in the 1850s, and the subsequent lifting of the ban on foreign travel, soon brought it to an end, but the advantages it gave

Above: Kaivopuisto Park and harbour view
Right: Observatory Hill

city itineraries

the city can still be seen. Just inside the park, down Iso Puistotie, is the attractive former Kaivohuone spa, dating from 1838; it now houses a restaurant.

Kalliolinnantie

Now follow the little road behind the car park, make a left turn onto Itäinen Puistotie and a right turn on Kalliolinnantie to an area of beautiful houses. To the left, at Kalliolinnantie 8, in a delightful wooden villa with an octagonal tower at one end and a wooden balcony on the top level, is one of the oldest art museums in Finland. The **Cygnaeus Gallery** (tel: 4050 9628; Wed 11am–7pm, Thur–Sun 11am–4pm; admission charge) opened in 1882. Its main exhibition consists of a 19th-century collection of Finnish art donated to the country by poet and critic Fredrik Cygnaeus (1807–81), professor of aesthetics and literature at Helsinki University.

Nearby, at Kalliolinnantie 14, is a more formidable building that belonged to one of Finland's most enigmatic men, the Marshal of Finland Baron Carl Gustav Mannerheim *(see page 15)*. The **Mannerheim Museum** (tel: 635 443; Fri–Sun 11am–4pm; admission charge) is housed in the Borman Villa, dating from 1873. Opened in 1951, and preserved as it was at Mannerheim's death, the exhibits include uniforms, medals and other personal memorabilia, as well as his extensive East Asian collections.

Further along, on the corner of Kalliolinnantie and Itäinen Puistotie, at No 7, is the most ornate of the Empire-style villas. It dates from 1839 and is the oldest preserved building in the park. Further down Itäinen Puistotie, behind strong fortifications, are the American, British and French embassies; only the British Ambassador's residence stands out architecturally.

Sea Views

At the end of the park, a small statue to the right honours Arvid Mörne (1876–1946) a Finnish poet who wrote in Swedish. Follow the road along the water to the right to the **Ursula Seaside Café**, whose array of mouthwatering sandwiches and shrimp and salmon delicacies may tempt you to linger on the canopied terrace admiring the small islands just offshore. Still following Ehrenströmintie, the jetties and the wooden racks on the shore present an unusual sight, but they had a purpose. Traditionally, people came here to the jetties to wash their carpets and dry them on the wooden racks.

Cobbled Merikatu, at the end of Ehrenströmintie, has more substantial buildings, and a right turn into Huvilakatu leads into a street of decorative Art Nouveau houses, which are some of the most attractive of their kind in the city. Take a left turn onto Tehtaankatu, and the dominant building straight ahead is the **Mikael Agricolan Church**, easily identified by its 30 m (98 ft) spire, one of the tallest in the city. As it was such a landmark during World

Right: the Mannerheim Museum

War II it was retracted back inside the tower to confuse the Russian bombers. Designed in a mix of Art Nouveau and classical styles, it was consecrated in 1935 and is named after the father of the Bishop of Turku and founder of the Finnish language.

Art and Architecture

Pass through the park surrounding the church towards a five-street junction just past the Old Skipper Pub, cross to a series of steps to the right, with children's playgrounds at each level, to reach a large, dignified church. Towards the end of the 19th century the growing population of Helsinki rendered the cathedral and the Old Church inadequate. It was decided that a larger church was required and between 1888 and 1891 the neo-Gothic silhouette of **St John's Church** (Johanneksen kirkko; Korkeavuorenkatu 12; tel: 709 2271; summer Mon–Fri noon–3pm, open Sun for mass at 10am) emerged on this hill. At the time it was the city's third Lutheran church, and with a capacity of 2,600 it is still the largest, dominated by the twin towers. The church stands on a spot where, for centuries, the people lit bonfires to celebrate midsummer, on 24 June. As this date is also Juhannus – St John the Baptist's Day – it gave the church its name. It has excellent acoustics and large choral concerts are sometimes held here, particularly Bach's *St Matthew Passion* on Easter Thursday.

Diagonally across from the main entrance is the little garden named **School Park**, with a sculpture by Ville Vallgren of *Topelius with Children*. Unveiled in 1909, it commemorates the writer, historian and storyteller Zacharias Topelius (1818–98). Across from the park, at Korkeavuorenkatu 23, is the grand façade of the **Design Museum** (Designmuseo; tel: 622 0540; www.designmuseum.fi; May–Aug daily 11am–6pm; Sept–Apr Tues 11am–8pm, Wed–Sun 11am–6pm; admission charge). The museum has a permanent exhibition of design objects from the second half of the 19th century to the present, complemented by temporary Finnish and international exhibitions.

Just behind, at Kasarmikatu 24, is the **Museum of Finnish Architecture** (Suomen Rakennustaiteen museo; tel: 8567 5100; www.mfa.fi; Tues, Thur–Sun 10am–4pm, Wed 10am–8pm; admission charge) in a neo-Renaissance building that was originally constructed for the Learned Societies in 1899.

Above: St John's Church
Right: the Design Museum

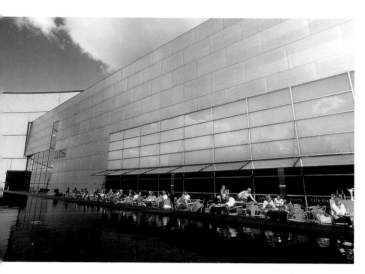

3. MANNERHEIMINAUKIO AND
SEURASAARI *(see map, p18–19)*

This tour takes in an impressive array of buildings and museums along Mannerheiminaukio, then heads out of the centre to the Olympic Stadium, with its fine views. After lunch, we see the Sibelius Monument then head for the Seurasaari Open-Air Museum.

Start at Central Railway Station. The tour includes a ride on the No 24 bus so bring your Tourist Ticket or Helsinki Card (see page 85).

Mannerheiminaukio

Make a right turn from the front entrance of the station and go past the modern post office to the futuristic building that is home to the **Kiasma, Museum of Contemporary Art** (Kiasma, Nykytaiteen museo; Mannerheiminaukio 2, tel: 1733 6501; www.kiasma.fi; Tues 9am–5pm, Wed–Sun 10am–8.30pm; admission charge, but free Fri 5–8.30pm and for under-18s). Kiasma is derived from the Greek word meaning crossing point and this strikingly modern museum was designed to maximise the light entering the building; even the fluorescent lights are set in special 'light pockets' to provide indirect illumination. Besides exhibiting Finnish and international contemporary art, one of the main purposes of this museum is to act as a public meeting place, with the aim of creating a lively, continuous contact between contemporary art and art lovers.

Directly outside is an impressive equestrian statue of Marshal Mannerheim *(see page 15)*, which was unveiled in 1960. Beside it is a pond from where water cascades down to a lower level behind the museum.

Mannerheimintie has some majestic buildings on either side of it – mainly modern on one side and traditional on the other. At No 30, the impressive rectangular building of red Finnish granite, with 14 columns and a wide set of steps, is the **Finnish Parliament Building** (guided tours all year: Sat

Above: the Kiasma, Museum of Contemporary Art

11am and noon, Sun noon and 1pm; Jul–Aug: also Mon–Fri 2pm). Constructed in 1931, this is arguably the best-known building in Finland, and is where the 200 members of the Eduskunta, the Finnish legislature, meet. When in session their deliberations can be viewed on Tuesday and Friday. Outside, at the foot of the steps, are statues of three of Finland's presidents.

Next, at No 34, is the eye-catching, irregular façade and tower of the **National Museum of Finland** (Suomen kansallismuseo; tel: 40 501; www.nba.fi/natmus; Tues–Wed 11am–8pm, Thur–Sun 11am–6pm; admission charge, but free Tues 5.30–8pm). The strikingly original National-Romantic façade, dating from the early 1900s, is meant to represent a combination of Finnish medieval churches and castles, along with a dash of Art Nouveau. A stone bear, Finland's symbol, stands guard outside the huge metal doors and inside, paintings depicting various stages of the country's history decorate the dome. The exhibits detail the development of Finnish life from the prehistoric era to present times, and are divided into five departments. The **Prehistory of Finland** is the country's largest permanent archaeological exhibition; the **Treasure Troves** is a sparkling collection of coins, medals, decorations, silver and weapons; the **Realm** details the history of Finnish culture and society; **A Land and its People** documents rural life in Finland before industrialisation; and the **Past Century** features independent Finland and its culture during the 20th century.

Cross back over Mannerheimintie and slightly to the right is the only older building on that side of the road. The attractive pink Hakasalmi Villa, which is now a branch of the City Museum, seems a little out of place here. It was built in 1846 and was once the home of a wealthy benefactor, Aurora Karamzin, who died here in 1902.

Next door, at No 13, is the modernistic **Finlandia Hall** (tel: 40 241; www. finlandia.hel.fi; closed except for guided tours and events; information shop open Mon–Fri 9am–4.30pm). Designed by the great Finnish architect Alvar Aalto in 1962 and built in 1967–71, this is Finland's most important concert and congress hall. It is both ornamental and functional and its marble walls bring a Mediterranean element to this northern land. The two halls are separated by a model of a church, also by Aalto, in Detmerode, Germany.

Next to the hall is the small **Hakasalmi Park**. Its main feature is a stainless-steel pool that is illuminated from below; in which the water is constantly circulated and heated in winter to prevent it from freezing. The four bronze

hands on top of high posts behind the pool are a monument to Urho Kaleva Kekkonen, President of Finland from 1956 to 1981, whose name is engraved in a rock behind the pool. The president was known for using his hands to express himself, and even wrote by hand rather than with a typewriter or word processor.

Above: outside the Parliament Building
Left: exhibits in the National Museum

Töölönlahti Bay and the Olympic Stadium

A pathway runs through Hesperia Park by the side of Töölönlahti Bay. As well as human fishermen, you are likely to see black-headed gulls that hover like hummingbirds before diving for fish. At the end of the park is another impressive modern structure – considered Finnish architecture at its finest. Regular opera performances were held in Finland for 120 years before the **Finnish National Opera** (Helsinginkatu 58; tel: 403 021; www.operafin.fi) moved to its new home here in 1993. There are performances of opera or ballet, or orchestral concerts, six nights a week, and the Finnish National Opera stages the world premier of at least one Finnish opera every season.

Moving on to the end of Töölönlahti Bay, the next stop is the **City Winter Garden** (Hammarskjöldintie, tel: 166 5410; Tues 9am–3pm, Wed–Fri noon–3pm, Sun 12–4pm; free), a particularly peaceful haven. Established in 1893 it is a combination of a small formal garden with statuary, and with pheasants running around, and a large, decorative greenhouse featuring an alluring combination of exotic plants, a fish pond and pieces of modern art.

The most dominant structure by far is the 72 m (236 ft) tower of the **Olympic Stadium** (tel: 436 6010; www.stadion.fi; tower visits: Mon–Fri 9am–8pm, Sat–Sun 9am–6pm; admission charge), and a visit to the two-level caged-in observation platform is recommended. The views are, quite simply, the finest in Helsinki and offer a panoramic perspective of not only the city, but the archipelago that surrounds it. Finland participated in the international Olympian movement before becoming an independent country in 1917, and it was their excellent results in the Olympic Games of the 1920s that led to dreams of holding the games in Helsinki. First, though, it was necessary to design and construct a stadium and this, then considered one of the most beautiful in the world, was inaugurated on 2 June 1938. However, because of World War II, it was not until 1952 that it played host to the XV Olympic Games, at which time it set its capacity record of

Above: a garden game of chess

70,435. These days, it seats just 40,000 people, who come to watch international sporting and musical events.

Also within the stadium complex is the **Sports Museum of Finland** (Urheilumuseo; tel: 434 2250; www.urheilumuseo.fi; Mon–Fri 11am–5pm, Sat–Sun noon–4pm; admission charge). It has 30,000 exhibits and more than 200,000 photographs depicting the great moments – of both victory and defeat – in the history of Finnish athletics. Multimedia and video shows add to the excitement, and bring the events to life. In front of the stadium a statue of Paavo

Nurmi (1897–1973) celebrates one of the greatest of all Finnish runners.

For lunch, walk to **Café Carelia**, a stylish modern restaurant across from the Opera House, where the menu specialises in mussel-based dishes *(see page 74)*.

A bit of exercise is now in order. Go three blocks down Runeberginkatu, a block up Topeliuksenkatu and then one more block eastwards along Sibeliuksenkatu and you will come to a small park. This is the location of the famous **Sibelius Monument**, a modern kinetic sculpture made of upright, organ-like metal pipes that resonate musically. It was created by Eila Hiltunen in 1967 as a memorial to the revered Finnish composer, Jean Sibelius, whose most famous work, *Finlandia*, was adopted by the Finnish people to represent pride and patriotism in the country's struggles against Russia.

Seurasaari Open-Air Museum

Now hop on a northbound No 24 bus on Mechelininkatu, which will take you away from the city on a pretty route around the waterside. On the left there will be a passing view of the house of the Finnish president, while on the right, along Seurasaarentie, you will see an elegant, cream-coloured house surrounded by red fences. The modern sculptures in the garden are indicative of the fact that four families of artists have occupied the house for several years.

The bus route ends a short distance further on, by the bridge that leads over to the park-like island location of the appealing **Seurasaari Open-Air Museum** (tel: 4050 9660 in summer, 4050 9574 in winter; Jun–Aug daily 11am–5pm; late May and early Sept Mon–Fri 9am–3pm, Sat–Sun 11am–5pm; admission charge). The museum was founded in 1909 and has 86 traditional buildings – cottages, farmsteads, a church and parsonage and a manor house – from all Finland's provinces, which give visitors a perspective of Finnish rural life from the 18th to the 20th century. Guides in traditional costumes demonstrate craft skills and folk dancing, shops and a restaurant sell typical products. A huge bonfire initiates the Midsummer Eve celebrations that are held here.

Above: high diving at the Olympic Swimming Stadium

Temppeliaukio Church and the Natural History Museum

Take the No 24 bus again to the junction with Arkadiankatu, and then walk east for a short distance to Helsinki's most unusual church and one of the city's most famous tourist attractions. The **Temppeliaukio Church** (Temppeliaukion kirkko; at Lutherinkatu 3, tel: 2340 5900; open most days but times vary; call for details) was built in 1968–69 by the architect brothers Timo and Tuomo Suomalainen. The walls have been quarried out of natural bedrock and it is topped by a massive copper dome with a diameter of 24m (79ft). It is lined with 22km (13 miles) of copper stripping, supported by reinforced concrete beams, and light is reflected inwards from 180 skylights. Also called the Church of the Rock, it can hold a congregation of 940 and has excellent acoustics, so try to visit during a service or attend one of the musical performances that are held here.

From the church, walk back down Fredrikinkatu to Arkadiankatu, noting along the way a coin-like memorial plaque to Jeorg Malnstn (1902–81). Also known as Georg Malmsten, he was Finland's most popular light entertainer in the years between the two world wars. A left turn on this street, which is divided by a lower-level railway line, leads to Pohjoinen Rautatienkatu and the distinguished neobaroque façade of the **Natural History Museum** (Luonnontieteellinen museo; tel: 191 28800; Tues–Fri 9am–5pm, Sat–Sun 11am–4pm; admission charge). The huge stone moose outside gives an indication as to what to expect inside, as does a model elephant facing you in the first hall.

From here it is just a short walk across Mannerheimintie back to Central Railway Station.

Above: the bridge to Seurasaari island
Right: farmstead at Seurasaari Open-Air Museum

4. PARKS, GARDENS AND A HARBOUR CRUISE
(see map, p18–19)

This morning trip takes you through the Botanical Gardens and across the Long Bridge to the Hakaniemi Indoor and Outdoor Market, then up Helsinki's longest street to the towering Kallio Church. Pretty Lenininpuisto Park offers the dual attractions of the Linnanmäki Amusement Park and the informative Merimaailma Sea Life Helsinki Aquarium. Then it's time for a cruise and a different perspective of the city.

Start at the Central Railway Station and come prepared with your Tourist Ticket or Helsinki Card to pay for the tram ride. Contact Royal Line (tel: 0207 118333) in advance to book your harbour cruise.

Head east from the station and pass behind the grand Finnish National Theatre, via a park area with a pond, statues and the Tomb of the Freemason, Fredrik Granatenhjelm, an officer of the Finnish artillery. The iron fence surrounding the memorial stone is hung with field artillery insignia. You'll soon come to an oasis of green and tranquillity in the heart of the city. The **Helsinki University Botanical Gardens Kaisaniemi** (Unioninkatu 44, tel: 1912 4453; garden, Apr–Sept Mon–Fri 7am–8pm, Sat–Sun 9am–8pm; Oct–Mar Mon–Fri 7am–5pm, Sat–Sun 9am– 5pm; free; greenhouses, Apr–Sept Tues–Sun 10am–5pm; Oct–Mar Tues–Sun 10am–3pm; admission charge). The garden was established in Turku, the old capital, in 1678 and transferred to Kaisaniemi Park – Helsinki's oldest – in 1829. Once through the gates, between wooden buildings, it consists of a formal garden with several 1830s Empire-style buildings and a series of greenhouses, the largest of which is the 1889 Palm House, which was renovated in 1998. The plants – nearly 3,000 varieties – are grouped according to their family or origin; they are labelled white for basic plants, red for endangered ones, and yellow for edible and medicinal types.

Hakaniemi Market

Now cross the Long Bridge – actually rather short – which was built in 1910–12, and enter an interesting, working-class area. To the left of McDonalds you will see the statue of *The Boxers* by Johannes Haapasalo, and in the large square to the right is **Hakaniemi Market** (Mon–Sat 7am–2pm), with an enticing array of products ranging from vegetables and fish to wicker furniture. There are also some of the little, tented cafés that are so popular in Finland. The market hall itself is two storeys, with food on the lower level, and an array of textiles and souvenirs upstairs. Unlike the Old Market Hall by Market Square, this one caters more to local people than to tourists. Immediately behind it is a local landmark, a triangular-shaped structure with round towers at each end that is home to the Comedy Theatre.

Above: ornamental detail in the University Botanical Gardens Kaisaniemi

Kallio Church

The most dominant landmark is straight ahead on top of the hill, reached by the longest street in Helsinki, Siltasaarenkatu. Before starting the climb, note the unusual memorial to the left at the first intersection. It consists of a leaning 8 m (26 ft) steel tower and a 7.5 m (24½ ft) slab of grey Kuru granite, with reliefs depicting women at work in homes, factories and farms, and is the first national memorial honouring the work done by women during World War II.

The tall, granite, Art Nouveau tower of **Kallio Church** (Kallion kikko) is most impressive, and sits on one of Helsinki's highest spots. Consecrated on 1 September 1912, it is the only church in Finland that has both baroque and French Romantic organs. It also has seven bells, and Sibelius composed a melody specially for them; it was used by the Finnish Broadcasting Company for a number of decades, when they were rung on Saturday evening.

In the morning (except on Sundays) you may see a queue of people along Papinkuja, directly across from the church. They are lining up for free bread from the Salvation Army – Finland is an affluent country, but pockets of poverty do exist, and this is one of them.

Lenininpuisto and Linnanmäki

From the church, take Alppikatu and then turn right at Kirstinkatu down to Helsinginkatu, the main road. Straight ahead, to the left, is a flyover, so you have to walk up through a small park by the side of the road to meet Sturenkatu. A diversion to the right brings you to a strange-looking red-brick building, the Kulttuuritalo, a concert hall famed for its acoustics. Inconspicuous behind a small car park is the entrance to **Lenininpuisto**, a pleasant little park. Initially, this was just a rocky outcrop, but what you see today, interspersed with streams, is an array of trees and shrubs – many not typically Finnish – that came from a garden exhibition in 1961–62. You

Above: summer fruits in Hakaniemi Market

may also be lucky enough to catch a glimpse of red squirrels – far more attractive than their grey cousins.

The park leads, via another car park, to the last two attractions of the morning. At Tivolikuja 1 is **Linnanmäki Amusement Park** (tel: 773 991, www.linnanmaki.fi; late-Apr–early Sept: daily variable hours; free, but charge for individual rides, priced according to your height). It is a fully

fledged amusement park with a good selection of rides. The park's neighbour, **Merimaailma Sea Life Helsinki** (tel: 565 8200; Oct–Apr and Sept–Dec Mon–Sun except Wed 10am–5pm, Wed 10am–8pm, May–Aug Mon–Sat 10am–7pm, Sun 10am–5pm; admission charge), is fairly small, but it has been extremely well designed and the exhibits are interesting for visitors of all ages. Feeding times (12.30pm and 2.30pm) are especially popular.

Harbour Cruise

From Linnanmäki Amusement Park/Merimaailma Sea Life Helsinki, you can take a No 3B tram directly to Market Square, the departure point for the harbour cruise – vessels leave from the end closest to the Havis Amanda fountain. You can take just the basic boat ride or, for an extra charge, have lunch on board as well.

Royal Line (Pohjoisranta 4, tel: 0207 118333; www.royalline.fi; early May–end Sept; advance booking advisable) offers the 'Helsinki City Tour and King's Gate', a cruise around the archipelago, with views of the Suomenlinna Fortress *(see page 43)* and Helsinki; lunch and dinner cruises in the archipelago are also available. One of the facts you will learn en route is that the salinity of the water here is so low that it doesn't support shrimps and mussels. Nevertheless, there are more than 60 species of fish in the waters, which in summer can reach a temperature of 20°C (68°F), but in winter freeze so hard that you can drive a car onto the ice. Boat trips last 1½ hours; dinner cruises 2½ hours.

5. BULEVARDI AND THE WATERSIDE *(see map, p18–19)*

This tour offers a mixed-bag of attractions: a walk along one of Helsinki's nicest streets, museums, an old wooden church in a pretty park, an open-air flea market and a walk around the water towards the city's newest cultural attraction – the Cable Factory (Kaapeli).

Start at Central Railway Station. The tour includes a tram ride.

Cross the road from the station and head past the Suurahuone Hotel, then cross Mannerheimintie and walk through The Forum shopping centre court-yard and up three sets of steps to emerge on Yrjönkatu. Here you'll find the **Amos Anderson Art Museum** (tel: 684 4460; www.amosanderson.fi; Mon–Fri 10am–6pm, Sat–Sun 11am–5pm; admission charge), one of the largest private art collections in Finland. It is housed in the impressive 1913 home and offices of Amos Anderson (1878–1961), a businessman who owned several printing houses and *Hufvudstadsbladet* – the largest Swedish-language newspaper in Finland. He was an avid collector of 20th-century Finnish art, and this is on display, along with some other collections.

Next comes the Sokos Torni Hotel, one of the tallest buildings in the mostly low-rise city centre. It is worth taking a diversion up to the Ateljee Bar on the 12th floor, where the observation platforms offer panoramic views of the city centre. From here, continue along Yrjönkatu and note the relief of a man on a horse, entitled the *Unexpected Visitor*, on a corner of one of the buildings.

The Old Church

On the corner with Lönnrotinkatu is a beautiful park and an interesting church, the oldest one in Helsinki. From the early 18th century to 1829 the park acted as a cemetery, and an outbreak of plague in 1710 resulted in half of Helsinki's population being buried here. There are 48 tombstones

Left: amusements at Merimaailma Sea Life Helsinki and Linnanmäki Amusement Park. **Above:** a wedding at the Old Church

and some important monuments, including a crypt designed by C L Engel for Johan Sederholm, a wealthy Helsinki merchant and ship owner.

The **Old Church** (Vanha kirkko; tel: 2340 6128; summer: Mon–Fri noon–3pm) takes pride of place. Consecrated on 17 December 1826, it was designed by Engel in neoclassical style, with a cruciform layout. A simple, gilded wooden cross, also designed by Engel, hangs behind the altar. Because the church was only intended to be for temporary use, until the new cathedral was ready, it was constructed with massive logs and was not even given any bells. However, the city's population had increased so much by the time the cathedral was consecrated in 1852 that the Old Church was retained as a permanent place of worship.

Bulevardi and the Hietalahti Market

Bulevardi, on the other side of the park, is an impressive street, with many beautiful façades of what were private residences in the late 19th and early 20th centuries. At No 9, the Ekberg Café – with one of Helsinki's tastiest selections of cakes and biscuits – is the oldest in Helsinki, in operation since 1852. Further down, in its own cobbled block, is the elegant **Alexander Theatre**. Named after Tzar Alexander II, it was built voluntarily by Russian officer engineers and conscripted soldiers, and staged its first performance in 1879. In 1918 it became the home of the Finnish Opera, which opened on 19 January 1919 with a performance of Verdi's *Aida*.

The end of Bulevardi used to be the home of the Sinebrychoff brewery, Finland's oldest, dating from 1819. It moved out in the early 1990s, but the Sinebrychoff name – they were a family of Russian merchants – is preserved both in the adjacent park and the **Sinebrychoff Art Museum** (Sinebrychoffin taidemuseo; tel: 1733 6460; Tues and Fri 10am–6pm, Wed–Thur 10am–8pm,

Sat–Sun 11am–7pm; admission charge). This three-storey, Empire-style house was donated to the state by Paul and Fanny Sinebrychoff in 1921, along with its collections of Old Flemish, Dutch, Italian and French paintings, Swedish portraits, Russian icons, silver, china and antique furniture.

Directly across the road, **Hietalahti Market Hall** (Mon–Fri 8am–6pm, Sat 8am–4pm) is a recently renovated Art Nouveau structure, which has an enticing array of produce. The attractive, wooden-roofed **Ravintola Knossos** offers a tempting daily lunch menu. Outside, in summer, you will find just about everything up to, and including, the kitchen sink at **Hietalahti Flea Market** (mid-May–Aug Mon–Fri 8am–2pm, Sat 8am–3pm, Sun 10am–4pm).

Along the Waterside

The waterside now beckons, with views of the massive shipbuilding yards across the bay. Walk around, passing the Radisson SAS Seaside Hotel, to a glass building with a shape like a ship's bow and, at Itänerenkatu, jump on a No 8 tram for two stops to the end of the line. There, you will see a giant black modern sculpture, and it is just one block to Tallberginkatu 1, home of the **Cable Factory** (Kaapeli; tel: 4763 8300; www.kaapelitehdas.fi), one of Helsinki's newest attractions. In converted U-shaped warehouses by the water, you will find an array of cultural and sports facilities that include ceramics, dance, theatres, galleries, art and architectural schools, an adult education centre, martial arts clubs, the Helsinki Athletes Club and three esoteric museums. It is a splendid social centre, of which Helsinki is proud.

If you didn't lunch at Ravintola Klossos, you could eat here at **Ravintola Hima & Sali**, a modern café with Internet access and a pleasant bar with sandwiches and snacks.

6. SUOMENLINNA FORTRESS *(see map, p44)*

A visit to an immense historical structure, on a series of small islands guarding the approaches to the city, plus museums, a church/lighthouse and art galleries.

Depart from Market Square for the 15-minute ferry ride to the fortress. On arrival, call in at the terminal shop and pick up a copy of the colourful and practical guide to the islands – attractions are diverse and far apart and paths are rather rough and poorly marked.

By the middle of the 17th century Sweden had become one of the great European powers and its possessions, besides Finland, included Ingria, Estonia and Livonia, and most of Pomerania. However, in 1703 Peter the

Top Left: the Empire Room in the Sinebrychoff Art Museum
Left: the Cable Factory. **Above:** an antiques stall in Hietalahti Market Hall

Great founded the new Russian capital of St Petersburg and fortified its approaches with the naval base of Kronstadt. But successive wars saw Sweden lose much of its Baltic territories and, through the treaties of Nystad and Turku, the Russian frontier was brought much closer, posing more of a

threat. Fortunately, Sweden had forged a military alliance with France, which offered financial subsidies to fortify the Russian frontier. Consequently, the Swedish Diet – under orders from King Fredrik I – decided in 1748 to instigate the building of a new naval base that would not only protect shipping channels to Helsinki but also serve as a landing base for extra troops from Sweden.

The new fortress, occupying a series of small islands that protected the entrance to Helsinki harbour, was called Sveaborg – Sweden's Fortress (it was only renamed Suomenlinna in 1918) – and became the largest construction project ever undertaken by the country. Lieutenant-Colonel Augustin Ehrensvärd (1710–72), who was also an astute politician, a good organiser and an experienced fortress planner, was given the responsibility of overseeing the construction. He decided that, to keep the edifice hidden as much as possible from enemy view, it should be a bastion with low fortification devices. It took many thousands of Finnish workers some 40 years to complete the principal work – by which time the walls extended to a total of around

8km (5 miles), with enough room for 1,300 cannons. At the close of the 18th century, workers at the dry dock here constructed the vessels that formed a renowned archipelago fleet.

Ehrensvärd's influence spread in other ways, too; he received various plants from his friend, the botanist Carl von Linné (also known as Linnaeus), and after he planted them in his garden they spread across the fortress. Sixteen years after his death, Ehrensvärd was buried here and his godson, King Gustav III of Sweden, designed the ornamental monument himself and personally laid the vault's keystone, using a silver trowel.

Above: aboard the ferry to Suomenlinna Market

Map labels

Merisotakoulu (The Naval Academy)

Suomenlinna

Pikku-Musta

Suomenlinnan Panimo (Suomenlinna Brewery)

Café Viaporin Kahvihuone

Suomenlinnan kirkko (Suomenlinna Church)

SUOMENLINNA

Länsi-Musta

Café Bar Valimo

Varvilahti

Sotamuseo "Maneesi" (The Military Museum "Manege")

Nukke-ja lelumuseo (Doll and Toy Museum)

Café Chapman

Suomenlinna-museo (Suomenlinna Museum)

Tullimuseo (Customs Museum)

Ehrensvärd-museo (The Ehrensvärd Museum)

Sukellusvene Vesikko (Submarine Vesikko)

Café Piper

Rannikkotykistömuseo (The Coastal Artillery Museum)

The King's Gate

Walhalla Restaurant

Suomenlinna

400 m / 440 yds

Military Action

By 1806, around 4,600 people were living on Sveaborg (Suomenlinna), making it the second-largest city in Finland after Turku, which was then the capital. Following an agreement between Alexander I of Russia and Napoleon, Russia occupied Finland in 1808, and under the Treaty of Hamina the following year Finland became an autonomous duchy within the Russian Empire, ending a 600-year period of Swedish rule. It was the presence of this fortress that prompted the Russians to decide on Helsinki as the new capital of Finland in 1812.

More than 12,000 troops were garrisoned in the fortress, along with their families and all the necessary support personnel, and there followed a long period of peace. However, this was shattered by the Crimean War of 1854–56, during which an Anglo-French fleet shelled and badly damaged the fortress over a period of three days. After the war, extensive restoration work was undertaken, with new defensive work on the western and southern edges of the islands, and in the build up to World War I the fortress and surrounding islands were incorporated into naval fortifications designed to protect St Petersburg.

After Finland gained its independence in 1918, Sveaborg was given its new name, Suomenlinna – Finland's Fortress – and its first, grisly use was as a death camp for the Reds (communists) who had lost the Finnish Civil War. It was then utilised as a closed military zone until 1948, and it was not until 1973 that Suomenlinna received a civilian administration. In 1991 the fortress was put on the UNESCO list of World Heritage Sites, in recognition of the fact that this fortress is an excellent and unique example of military architecture.

Artistic Enclave

Despite its military purpose, Suomenlinna has always been known as a place of avant-garde culture, where the arts, music and theatre have flour-

Above: Lieutenant-Colonel Augustin Ehrensvärd's tomb in Castle Yard

ished, an environment assisted by the large numbers of officers stationed there. Augustin Ehrensvärd himself was the first Suomenlinna artist, and others included Elias Martin and A E Gete, who lived here in the 1760s and whose works depict daily life at the time. On the musical front, Bernhard Henrik Crusell, a composer and clarinettist, began his career as a student in the military band, in 1787.

Today, many artists live permanently on Suomenlinna. There are a number of studios and galleries on the islands and the Nordic Institute for Contemporary Art manages five guest studios. Theatre also flourishes, and the summer theatre staged at the bastion of Hyvä Omatunto – meaning Good Conscience – regularly sells out its performances.

There are around 900 civilians living on the islands now, of whom about 350 work here year round, while the rest commute to Helsinki. They all enjoy a privileged position, being close to the centre of Helsinki yet removed from city stresses on their own idyllic islands.

Suomenlinna's Museums

A visit to Suomenlinna is also enhanced by a fine array of museums. The most important of these is **Suomenlinna Museum** (Building C74, tel:684 1880; May–Sept daily 10am–6pm; Jan–Apr and Oct–Dec daily 10am–4pm; admission charge). Located in the navy's former inventory chambers, it doubles as the information centre and details the history of the fortress from the 18th century to the present. Don't miss the multimedia show, 'The Suomenlinna Experience', which is broadcast hourly in the museum auditorium.

One of the oldest houses in the complex is the former Commandant's official residence, which was originally the home of the creator of the fortress. Fittingly, it now houses the **Ehrensvärd Museum** (Building B40, tel: 684 1850; Apr: Sat–Sun 11am–4pm; May–Aug daily 10am–5pm; Sept: daily 11am–4pm; Oct: Sat–Sun 11am–4pm; admission charge), and contains portraits, furnishings and model ships. Augustin Ehrensvärd's elaborate grave and monument are located in front of the house.

The Military Museum has three separate entities. The **Coastal Artillery Museum** (Rannikkotykistömuseo; Building A2, tel: 1814 5295; mid-May–Aug daily 11am–6pm; admission charge) is found in an 18th-century

gunpowder cellar on Kustaanmiekka Island and exhibits coastal defence equipment used over the past 300 years. The **Manege** (Maneesi; Building C77, tel: 1814 5296; mid-May–Aug daily 11am–6pm; admission charge) features heavy military equipment – most of which dates from the World War II era, in a building that was constructed by the Russians in 1881. The ***Submarine Vesikko*** (*Sukellusvene Vesikko*; Building B79, tel: 1814 6238; mid-May–Aug daily 11am– 6pm; admission charge) is the only surviving submarine that served in the Finnish fleet from 1936–47, and worked the Gulf of Finland during World War II.

A more gentle experience can be found at the **Doll and Toy Museum** (Nukke-ja lelumuseo; Building C66, tel: 668 417) where, in an old Russian villa, there is a collection of dolls and toys dating from the 1830s onwards. There's also a small café, should you need a break for refreshment.

Suomenlinna Church

Not to be missed is the **Suomenlinna Church** (Suomenlinnan kirkko; Wed–Thur 12–4pm), which was inaugurated in 1854 as the Alexander Nevsky Orthodox Church. Originally, it had five towers with onion domes but when, in 1928, it changed alliances and became a Lutheran church, four of the towers were demolished and the main one rebuilt in neo-Gustavian style, that is, consistent with the style introduced by Gustav III in the late 18th century. It has a lighthouse-type beacon. Its bell is the largest in Finland and the fence, made of cannon and chains, was erected in the 1850s.

Where to Eat

There is an eclectic array of places to eat on Suomenlinna. The **Suomenlinna Brewery**, a mix of restaurant and brewery pub, has a sunny garden and is located in the Jetty Barracks next to the ferry harbour. Just a short walk away, in the Russian merchants' quarter, is the small **Viapori Coffee Room**, which specialises in home-made pastries. The Adlerfelt traverse, built in 1770 near the Artillery Bay, houses the **Café Chapman**, which has a summer terrace. Nearby, in a 19th-century building originally used for casting ammunition, is the **Café-Bar Valimo** (summer only). Another option is the **Café Piper** (summer only), set in a park; dating from 1928 it replaced old garden pavilions and a Catholic chapel. It is about halfway between the Café Chapman and the **Restaurant Walhalla** on the tip of the island of Kustaanmiekka, at the south of Suomenlinna. This is a combination of gourmet restaurant, bar and the Pizzeria Nikolai – named after Nikolai Sinebrychoff, who founded the oldest brewery in the Nordic countries.

Left: taking a bracing walk around Suomenlinna Fortress
Above: exhibit in the Ehrensvärd Museum

Excursions

This section gives details of four excursions that are easily made from Helsinki and offer a broad view of Finland's history and culture. The fourth tour crosses the border into Estonia.

1. PORVOO (BORGÅ) *(see map, p50)*

Finland's second-oldest town, once a prominent medieval trading centre, preserves some picturesque old buildings, and has several interesting museums, speciality shops and a fine cathedral, sitting majestically on the hill between the Market Square and the riverside.

There are frequent bus services from the bus station in Helsinki to the market square in Porvoo, with a journey time, depending upon traffic, of around an hour. Throughout the summer, there is also a ferry service, offering a pleasant alternative that takes about 3 hours (see Practical Information, page 86), but might mean you'd need to stay overnight to do it full justice.

Porvoo, about 50km (32 miles) east from Helsinki, was known as a trading place in the 13th century, but the settlement was founded in the middle of the 14th century and named after a castle (that no longer exists) beside the Linnamäki River. Finland was then ruled by Sweden and the place was named Borgå, from the Swedish words *borg* for castle and *å* for river. Like all medieval Finnish towns, Provoo's coat-of-arms has a letter motif: C from the Latin word for castle. It achieved affluence during the era when German merchants of the Hanseatic League traded from the ochre-red shore houses that so delight visitors today. However, the night of 11 June 1760 was a disaster for Porvoo when, as a result of a cooking fire, the whole town went up in flames and 202 of the 293 houses were destroyed.

A city of significance

Finland's 700-year association with Sweden came to an end after the war between Sweden and Russia in 1808–9, when Finland was annexed to Russia as an autonomous Grand Duchy. One of the most momentous occasions in Finnish history occurred when the Russian Tsar Alexander I convened the diet in Porvoo Cathedral on 29 March 1809, which ratified the religion and fundamental laws of the land as well as the rights of the Estates.

In the 19th century Porvoo became a haven for artists and today there are museums dedicated to local artists.

Left: view of Porvoo
Right: vintage travel

MRR·10

Empire-style District

The start of the tour is in **Tori Torget**, where the bus from Helsinki arrives. It is a small square that doubles as a market place (Mon–Sat 7am–2pm). On the side that leads down to the river there is a little park and half-way down is a statue of Johan Ludvig Runeberg, the national poet, who wrote the lyrics for the national anthem – *Maamme (Our Country)*. Turn left here and, after crossing Raatihuoneenkatu, follow Runeberginkatu to Aleksanterinkatu where you will find two houses of real interest.

The first of these, at Aleksanterinkatu 3, is the **J L Runeberg Home** (tel: 58 13 30; May–Aug Mon–Sat 10am–4pm, Sun 11am–5pm; Sept–Apr Wed–Sat 10am–4pm, Sun 11am–5pm; admission charge), where Runeberg lived with his wife from 1852 until his death 25 years later. In 1882 it was opened as a museum, and the interior remains unchanged from that time. On the next block, at No 5, is a memorial to Runeberg's son, Walter (1838–1920), who was skilled in a different art form. **Walter Runeberg's Sculpture Collection** (tel: 58 21 86; May–Aug Mon–Sat 10am–4pm, Sun 11am–5pm; Sept–Apr Wed–Sun 11am–3pm; combined admission charge with the J L Runeberg Home) consists of around 140 of his works. He was born in Porvoo but worked in Paris and Rome for more than 30 years. The statue of his father that stands in the park is one of his works, and a similar, larger one is on display in the capital.

This Empire-style district follows a clear, rectangular, street layout similar to that around the Senate Square in Helsinki. It evolved between 1825 and 1855, when Tzar Nicholas I tried to lessen the density of the houses, and the danger of fire, by creating this regular, spacious plan. Fortunately, though, he didn't get around to including the Old Town. Follow Aleksanterinkatu down to the riverfront; it is on the quayside here that the boats to and from Helsinki dock. There is also a tourist information kiosk (late June–end Aug Mon–Sun 11am–5pm).

Walk alongside the river to the bridge that carries the main road from Helsinki into Porvoo and stop at the **tourist office** at Rihkamakatu 4, to stock up on information about the town; then break for lunch at the nearby **Porvoon Paahtimo** (Mannerheiminkatu 2), one of the attractive old red buildings beside the river.

Porvoo

200 m / 220 yds

- - - - Itinerary E1

Kankurinkuja · Kirkkokatu · Tuomiokirkko (Cathedral) · Valkatu · Kulmakuja · Edelfelt-Vallgren-museo (Edelfelt-Vallgren Museum) · Historiallinen museo (History Museum) · Porvoo Doll and Toy Museum (Nukke-ja lelumuseo) · Outboard Museum · Mannerheiminkatu · Silianpää · Vuorikatu · Valkatu · Rihkamakatu · Papinkatu · Raatihuoneenkatu · Runeberginkatu · Raatihuoneenkatu · Mannerheiminkatu · Raatihuoneenkatu · Raatihuoneenkatu · Lundinkatu · Bus Station · Tori Torget · Kaupungintalo (Town Hall) · Piispankatu · Raatihuoneenkatu · Aleksanterinkatu · Raatihuoneenkatu · Walter Runebergin veistoskokoelma (Walter Runeberg's Sculpture Collection) · JL Runebergin Koti (JL Runeberg's Home) · Lukiokatu · Kokonniementie · Nase · Jutten katu · Porvoonjoki · Lundinkatu · Helsinki

Porvoo's Museums

When you are ready to resume the tour, turn onto Jokikatu for a really pleasant surprise. This small, cobbled street is home to some attractive wooden buildings that house an array of speciality, craft and souvenir shops. It is along here that

you really begin to feel the ambience of this unusual little town, especially when you wander among the old shore houses and granary buildings (many of which are private dwellings) that back onto the river. One of these granaries now houses the **Outboard Museum** (Jokikatu 14; tel: 811 134; June–mid-Aug Sat–Sun 11am–3pm) where you can learn how an outboard repair shop operated in the middle of the 19th century. In the inner courtyard is the **Porvoo Doll and Toy Museum** (Nukke–ja lelumuseo; tel: 582 941; www.lelumuseo.com; Jun–July Mon–Thur and Sat 11am–3.30pm, Sun noon–3.30pm; admission charge). The museum was founded in 1974 by Evi Söderlund, who spent around 35 years of her life researching this subject and donated her collection to the museum. It consists of more than 1,000 dolls and many hundreds of toys, collected from Finland and abroad, and is generally acclaimed as the best collection of its kind in the country.

Too soon, the street opens out into a small plaza dominated by a square, rococo-style building with an unusual central tower. This is the Old Town Hall (1764), regarded as the second most important building in Porvoo, after the cathedral, and one of only two 18th-century town halls in Finland. Today it is home to the interesting **History Museum** (tel: 574 7500; www.porvoonmuseo.fi; May–Aug Mon–Sat 10am–4pm, Sun 11am–4pm; Sept–Apr Wed–Sun noon–4pm; admission charge) which brings to life the way people used to live in Porvoo through displays of furniture, costumes, textiles, glass, porcelain and silver, as well as toys and vehicles,. There are also multimedia programmes illustrating life in the Middle Ages.

Next door, in an old merchant's house dating from 1762, is the **Edelfelt-Vallgren Museum** (hours as for History Museum; combined admission charge) displaying the works of two local men – Albert Edelfelt and Ville Vallgren – as well as paintings by other artists. The sculptor Vallgren (1855–1940) was a Porvoo native, but studied and worked in Paris for nearly 40 years. His most famous work is the statue of *Havis Amanda (see page 29)* erected in Helsinki in 1908. Edelfelt

Above: the pretty wooden buildings that typify Porvoo
Right: pointing the way in Porvoo

(1854–1905), who was also born in Porvoo, painted historical motifs and portraits, including many of the Russian imperial family. There are also works on display by Ragnar Ekelund, Johan Knutson and Nils Schillmark, as well as furniture and ceramics.

Porvoo Cathedral

Jokikatu eventually opens up, with the riverbank on the left and some much larger houses to the right; straight ahead is a bridge guarded by a cannon on the opposite bank. Still on the city side of the bridge, take the steep, cobbled Sillanmaki – difficult for cars and pedestrians alike – up to the most dominant structure in this part of town, **Porvoo Cathedral** (Tuomiokirkko; tel: 661 11; www.porvoonseurakunnat.fi; May–Sept Mon–Fri 10am–6pm, Sat 10am–2pm, Sun 2–4pm; Oct–Apr Tues–Sat 10am–2pm, Sun 2–4pm). The oldest sections date from the late 13th and early 14th centuries, but the exterior is mainly 15th-century, with a steeply angled roof typical of medieval churches of the area. Inside, little remains from those years. It was severely damaged by the Danes in the early 16th century, and by the Russians later that century, and was hit hard during the Great Northern War in 1708. It became a cathedral in 1723 when the Episcopal See was moved here from Viborg. Points of interest include a statue of Alexander I, erected in 1909 on the centenary of the Porvoo Diet; and a hanging ship that dates from 1990, replacing the 18th-century one now preserved in the National Museum. Interestingly, the bell tower is set to the side of the main building.

Return to your bus or ferry by way of Kirkkokatu, a street of lovely wooden houses on stone bases, crossing the main Helsinki road at the bottom.

2. TAMPERE *(see map, p54)*

A visit to Finland's first industrial city, a thriving modern city that grew out of a medieval market town.

The journey between Helsinki and Tampere on regular Inter-City trains take just under 2 hours.

Tampere owes its existence to the blessings of nature. It sits on a relatively narrow stretch of land between Lake Näsijärvi to the north, which empties its waters through the Tammerkoski rapids, with a drop of 18m (59ft) into Lake Pyhäjärvi to the south. As early as the 15th century this water power was utilised to operate the mills of affluent farmers. It wasn't until 1779, however, that the Swedish king, Gustav III, decreed that a market town should be founded on the western shore of the rapids, to the benefit of industry and trade. Following the war of 1808–9 when Russia assumed control of Finland, the privilege of free trade was reconfirmed by Alexander I, and again by Alexander III, in 1855.

In practice, this gave Tampere a licence to export products to Russia without having to pay customs duty.

Surprisingly, though, even as late as the 1830s only a few modest factory buildings existed here, and it wasn't until much later in the 19th century that most of the landmark industrial buildings seen today were erected. Over the course of the 19th century, the rapids were cleaned and narrowed several times, maximising their natural energy and making Tampere Finland's first industrial city. Many of the factories have long since closed, but their imposing buildings haven't been allowed to decay. Instead, they have been converted into offices, museums, restaurants and breweries, and, as a result, Tampere has not only retained its infrastructure but built upon it to create a thriving, modern, cultural city encased in a largely 19th-century body.

City squares

From the railway station, turn left along Rautatienkatu south to the **Orthodox Church** (Ortodoksinen kirkko; tel: 3141 2724; June–Aug Mon–Sat 11am–5pm, Sun noon–4pm; May Mon–Sat 10am–4pm). Constructed between 1896 and 1899, it is also known as St Alexander Nevski and as St Nicolas, and is considered one of the purest examples of a neo-Byzantine church in Scandinavia.

At the foot of a small park on Sori Square outside the church is an unusual granite statue dating from 1987 and called *Pirkka*. This symbolises the wooden currency used by the ancient people of the same name. The currency

Top Left: Porvoo's Old Town Cathedral. **Left:** bric-a-brac for sale, Porvoo
Right: the onion domes of the Orthodox Church, Tampere

was in two parts, each notched to mark the amount due. When payment was made, the two halves were matched together.

A right turn at the foot of the park will lead to the **tourist office**, housed in the former office building of the Vekatehdas wool factory, built in 1896 when the local textile industry was at its peak. From here, follow the river, cross the wooden bridge and pass through an archway into a courtyard that once belonged to the textile mill of Kehräsaari, now home

to a host of interesting boutiques. Immediately beyond is **Laukontori Square**, the market square and inland port for local boat cruises.

Lenin Museum

Follow Satamakatu to Hämeenpuisto, with a broad, central, tree-lined walkway originally designed as a firebreak. A right turn here will take you to the Theatre of Tampere and the Workers' Hall (TTT), at Hämeenpuisto 28. On the third floor of the latter is the **Lenin Museum** (tel: 212 3973; Mon–Fri 9am–6pm, Sat–Sun 11am–4pm; admission charge), the only one of its kind outside the Soviet Union when it opened in 1946 and now one of only two in the world, the other being a small one in St Petersburg. It was in the Workers' Hall here that Lenin pledged to further the cause of Finnish independence, and it was where Lenin met Stalin for the first time at a Russian Social Democratic Workers' Party Conference in December 1905.

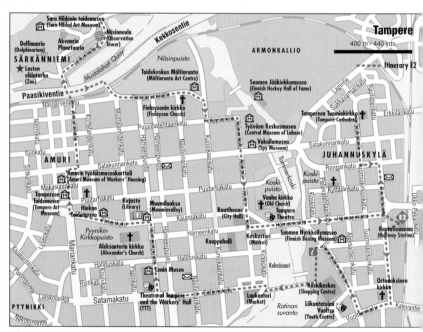

Leaving the museum, turn left onto Hämeenpuisto up **Pyynikin Church Park**, on the site of a cemetery that was established in 1785 and functioned as such until the late 1880s. To the right is **Alexander's Church**, whose foundation stone was laid on 2 March 1880, the 25th anniversary of Tzar Alexander II's ascension to the throne. Basically neo-Gothic in style, it incorporates other elements and has an altarpiece painted by Aleksandra Saltin in 1883.

Amuri Museum and the Observation Tower

Around the corner at Makasiininkatu 12 is the **Amuri Museum of Workers' Housing** (Amurin Työläismuseokortteli; tel: 3146 6634; May–mid-Sept: Tues–Sun 10am–6pm; admission charge), a fascinating example of workers' lifestyles in Tampere between the 1880s and the 1960s. The Amuri district's history dates back to 1779 when industrialisation brought more people to the town and the nobility had to give up land to house them (they named it after the Amur province in Siberia, to which many emigrants went in search of work). This was Finland's first workers' quarter, and at the turn of the 20th century about 5,000 people lived in these wooden dwellings, where four living chambers were built around a communal kitchen, with four separate fireplaces so each housewife could cook at the same time. With stables, saunas and running water, this became almost a self-contained community, with inhabitants obtaining food and other necessities from the co-operatives in the area, or from the Mustalahti market. Today it consists of five residential buildings and four outbuildings, all in their original locations; another, later outbuilding houses a mixed public sauna. There is also a cobbler's shop from 1906, a 1930s bakery and co-operatives, and a stationer and haberdashery.

The tour passes modern apartment blocks, then goes through a tunnel under the railway lines and, finally, across a busy road to one of the main attractions in Tampere, the **Näsinneula Observation Tower** (Särkänniemi; tel: 2488 111; www.sarkanniemi.fi; May–early Oct daily 10am–11.30pm; hours vary at other times; admission charge). It opened in 1971, and at a height of 168m (550ft), is the tallest observation tower in Finland, offering incredible views. On one side, the heavy industrialisation of Tampere is clearly seen, while on the other, lakes and forests stretch to the horizon.

Särkänniemi

A perfect place to stop for lunch in Tampere is at the revolving **Restaurante Näsinneula**. Besides offering great food, it turns completely in just under an hour, giving an amazing perspective of the city and surrounding countryside. The tower is in the middle of the huge **Särkänniemi Adventure Park** with an amusement park and children's zoo, the largest aquarium in Finland, with more than 200 species, a planetarium, the northernmost

Left: Laukontori Square, Tampere
Right: Alexander's Church

dolphinarium in the world and the **Sara Hildén Art Museum**, showing a collection of Finnish and foreign contemporary art.

Leaving this area, pass the **Mustalahti Quay**, now primarily a marina with pleasure craft and floating restaurants, then cross busy Kekkosentie and stroll along Näsijärvenkatu beside Näsinpuisto Park. At its heart is the sizeable neo-baroque Milavida Palace, seen to best advantage from the observation tower. Worth seeking out in the park is a 1913 fountain with three

sculptures symbolising the cycle of life and the interaction of generations. Round the corner, at Kuninkaankatu 2, is **Mältinranta Art Centre** (Taidekeskus Mältinranta; tel: 214 9214; Mon–Thur noon–6pm, Fri–Sun noon–4pm; free), established in 1982. It occupies a former water purification plant with attractive stable yards built by Wilhelm von Nottbeck, the first large-scale industrialist in Finland, who bought the Finlayson cotton mill in 1835. He had links with Russian nobility, and the stable yards were built of Russian wood with elaborate ornamentation. They have been restored and are unique in Finland.

Finlayson Complex and the Main Square

The name of Finlayson is prevalent in this area of Tampere. Close by is the beautiful **Finlayson Church**, low and elongated, without tower or spire. It was built in 1879 to serve the nearby Finlayson factory workers' housing area, which had been declared a separate and distinct parish. The **Finlayson factory area** was founded by James Finlayson in the 1820s to manufacture weaving machines. Later in that century, under Van Nottbeck, the business evolved into a large-scale cotton industry, spawning what became a town within a town. These historic factories now house the **Central Museum of Labour** (Työväen keskusmuseo; Väinö Linnan aukio 8; tel: 253 8800; www.tkm.fi), which specialises in the history and heritage of labour.

Outside the Finlayson complex, Tampere's main square is lined by interesting buildings, some in the Finnish Art Nouveau style. The attractive **Old Church**, dating from 1824, is the oldest public building in the town, its congregation mainly Lutheran Swedish residents. To the rear is **Tampere Theatre**, dating from 1913, and opposite this is the elegant façade of the **City Hall**

Above: the nave of Finlayson Church, Tampere
Right: Tampere's Old Church

(Raatihuone), built in 1890, and now used for civic receptions. The annual Independence Day address is read from its balcony on 6 December.

Tampere Cathedral

Walk along Hämeenkatu, the dividing line between the older and more modern parts of Tampere, towards the dominant brick tower of the railway station. Cross the wide **Hämeensilta Bridge**, completed in 1929 to commemorate the 150th anniversary of the town's foundation. Its four dominant statues represent a huntsman, a tradesman, a tax collector and a Finnish maiden.

From the station make a short diversion to see **Tampere Cathedral** (Tampereen Tuomiokirkko; Mon–Sun 9am–6pm; guided tours 11am–3pm), also known as St John's Church, which was built in the early 20th century and became a cathedral in 1923. The huge building has three towers of irregular height, topped with red-brick spires, and is protected by stone walls with six gateways, matching the towers in style. The altarpiece is by Symbolist artist Magnus Enckell (1870–1925), and other important Symbolist paintings adorn its walls.

3. TURKU (ÅBO) *(see map, p58)*

A visit to Turku, former capital and prominent in Finland's religious heritage, takes in the castle and cathedral, and some interesting museums and galleries, including a maritime centre.

The fast Pendolino train between Helsinki and Turku takes just under 2 hours. If you make an early start you will have time to see the most important sights in a day, as well as enjoying a walk along the riverbank.

Turku (Åbo in Swedish) has a long and illustrious history. In 1229 the Bishop's seat was moved here and this became the capital of the eastern part of Sweden. In 1280, work began on the formidable Turku castle, and by 1300 a stone church had been consecrated as the cathedral, but it wasn't until the late 15th century that it achieved the magnificence you will see today. In 1551 the then Bishop of Turku, Mikael Agricola, translated the New Testament into Finnish, and in 1640 Turku became the site of the country's first university. However, three years after Russia defeated Sweden in 1809, Helsinki became the new capital, and after the Great Fire of 1827 destroyed most of Turku, the university also moved to Helsinki.

Most of the city's attractions are located along either side of the Aura River, between the castle to the west and the cathedral to the east. The only exception is the Market Square, which is just a couple of blocks north. The

Above: stained-glass window in Tampere Cathedral

river itself is lined with hundreds of colourful vessels, some housing floating restaurants. For a city of its size, Turku has a wide range of museums, and numerous statues and other works of art adorn its attractive streets. The

town has a lively, open atmosphere, which is reflected in its restaurant scene, typified by the popular Viking Restaurant Harald.

Market Square to the River

From the railway station take a mini-bus taxi to lively **Market Square** (Kauppatori) where a fully fledged market (Mon–Sat 7am–2pm and weekday evenings in summer) has stalls selling a colourful array of meat, fish, produce, handicrafts and clothes. In the middle of June the square also plays host to the intriguing, four-day **Medieval Market** with almost 100 stalls with all kinds of medieval treats. Alongside this, there is a 4-hour **Market Play** during which actors in medieval costume mix with the onlookers and you can test your aim with a bow and arrow or sharpen up your swordsmanship. Of the buildings lining the square, the most impressive are the **Orthodox Church** (Yliopistonkatu; Apr–Aug daily 10am–3pm), which was built by order of

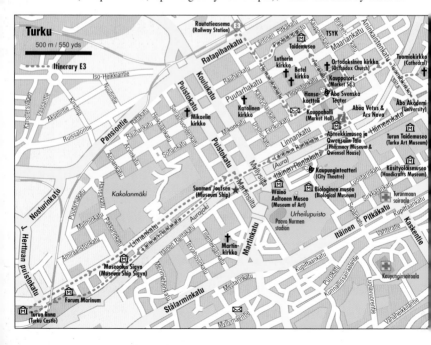

Emperor Nicolas I in 1838, and the **Åbo Svenska Teater** (Aurakatu 10; tel: 277 7377; www.abo.fi/teater), which dates from 1839. As well as being Finland's oldest theatre it is considered the most beautiful.

Next, you could stop at the **tourist office** for local information, then continue along Aurakatu to the river, where a right turn will lead to a beautiful, low-slung, red house at Läntinen Rantakatu 13 that is home to the **Pharmacy Museum and Qwensel House** (Apteekkimuseo ja Qwenselin Talo; tel: 262 0280; mid-Apr–mid-Sept daily 10am–6pm; rest of year Tues–Sun 10am–3pm; admission charge). Dating from around 1700, this is considered to be the oldest privately owned mansion in Turku and allows visitors an opportunity to glimpse the lifestyle of the affluent classes in the time when Finland was ruled by Sweden. The Gustavian style in which some of the rooms are decorated was introduced by Gustav III (1772–92). He had spent some time at the court of Versailles, and had been inspired by the French neoclassical style of architecture. The exhibits within the museum trace the history of the pharmacy from the beginning of the 19th century.

Along the Riverside to the Castle

The banks of the Aura River are a real delight, and the riverside walkway on the western bank is a pleasant way of reaching Turku's main attraction. Along the way, the ever-increasing maritime influence is reflected cleverly in the modernistic **Forum Marinum** (tel: 2829 511; www.forum-marinum.fi; May–Sept daily 11am–7pm; Oct–Apr Tues–Sun 10am–6pm; admission charge) at Linnankatu 72. Besides being a centre for maritime research, it has more than 3,500 exhibits relating to the maritime history of southwest Finland. It holds permanent exhibitions in the old Kruununmakasiini, the Crown Granary, dating from 1894, and temporary exhibitions in the Linnanpuomi building, which was originally built as a warehouse for the SOK Cooperative in the early 1930s. This is also the only maritime centre in the Nordic countries that has its own quay at the heart of a busy river and commercial port. During June, July and August a number of interesting ships can be inspected (daily 11am–7pm; admission charge). The 'Skipper Bracelet' is valid for a day and allows entrance to all exhibitions and museum ships. Rising from the water here is the graceful, modernistic *Harmonia* statue by Achim Kuhn.

Now head for the symbol of the city, the formidable **Turku Castle** (Turun Linna; Linnankatu 80, tel: 262 0300; Apr–Sept daily 10am–6pm; Oct–Mar Tues–Sun 10am–3pm; admission charge). This is one of Finland's most magnificent national treasures. It dates from around 1280, when, as the water level was higher then, it was situated on an island, and it grew over the next few cen-

Above: at the Pharmacy Museum, Turku
Right: Turku's Forum Marinum

turies to reach its apogee in the 16th century, during the reign of Duke Johan and Katarina Jagellonica. It was during this time that the Renaissance floor and the King's and Queen's halls were added. Looking just like a castle should, it is great fun to visit; one of its most popular parts is the prison of Erik XIV, who took the throne of Sweden in the 16th century but was later overthrown by his brother. The **Historical Museum** in the castle's bailey features permanent exhibitions about the history of Turku, with themed rooms showing dress, customs and interior decor from the 17th to the 19th century. Throughout the castle there are more displays of historical costumes, along with glass, porcelain and jewellery, while the simple, elegant chapel has medieval woodcarvings and votive ships.

Art and History Museums

Take the No 1 bus from the castle to Allegatan and cross the bridge to the east bank of the river, where the first place of interest is the **Wäinö Aaltosen Museum of Art** (tel; 262 0850; www.wam.fi; Tues–Sun, 11am–7pm; admission charge), just past the next bridge, at Rantakatu 38. This somewhat stark building was opened in 1967, primarily to exhibit the works – sculptures, paintings, graphics and drawings – of Wäinö Aaltosen (1894–1966), one of Finland's most prominent sculptors. The collection totals more than 4,500 works, many of them sited in public buildings around the city.

At the next bridge, cross over towards the town for a short diversion and lunch at the **Viikinkivintola Harald**, Aurakatu 3, one of Turku's most colourful and imaginative restaurants, both for its decor and cuisine.

Above: Turku Castle, dating from the 13th century
Right: a bright young Finn in Turku

Recross the bridge, and straight ahead on the Vartiovuorenmäki hill sits the unmistakable outline of what was once Carl Ludwig Engel's observatory. It is currently serving as the home of the **Turku Art Museum** (Turun taide-museo; tel: 262 7100; www.turuntaidemuseo.fi; Tues–Thur 11am–6pm, Fri–Sun 10am–4pm; admission charge) until it moves back to its original site, which is currently being renovated *(see page 62)*.

Down by the river again, just past the statue of the runner, Paavio Nurmi, the street changes its name to Hämeenkatu and, very soon, there is a dual attraction: the **Aboa Vetus** and the **Ars Nova** (tel: 250 0552; www.abo.fi; summer daily 11am–7pm; winter Tues–Sun 11am–7pm; separate or com-bined admission charges), comprising the **Museum of Archaeology and History** and the **Museum of Contemporary Art**, housed in the Rettig Palace. One of the main attractions of the former is the excavated city block of medieval Turku, complete with arched cellars and cobbled streets, that was only discovered accidentally in the early 1990s. The Museum of Contem-porary Art holds the collection of the Matti Kolvurinta Foundation, com-prising more than 500 20th-century works by leading artists from Finland and other countries. There is a good little shop and a small café. Note the memorial stone in the window on the river side of the building; it com-memorates Hernan Spöring (1733–71), a native of Turku who travelled with Captain James Cook between 1768 and 1771.

The Old Great Square and the Cathedral

The next stop is the most important square in Turku, known as the **Old Great Square**. Since the 13th century, this has been both the secular and ecclesiasti-cal heart of the city, with the old town hall and similarly majestic structures along one side and the imposing cathedral on the other. Today, the four most important buildings – the Brinkkala Mansion, the Old Town Hall, Hjelt Mansion and Juselius Mansion – have all been renovated, and combine to form the **Turku Cul-tural Centre**; it is from the specially constructed balcony of the former that the famous proclamation of Christmas Peace is read at midnight on 24 December each year. Among its many uses, the mansion has served

as the residence of the Russian Governor General. Note the special flag that flies over these buildings; the motif dates back to the 14th century and depicts a Gothic A – for Aboa Turku – and four lilies symbolising the Virgin Mary. Until the late 1880s this area also had a market, but today the mansions, yards and exte-rior areas are used for a variety of cultural events.

The immense tower of **Turku Cathedral and Cathedral Museum** (Turun Tuomiokirkko; tel: 261 7100; www.turunsrk.fi; Apr–Sept daily 9am–8pm; Oct–Mar 9am–7pm; cathedral free, admission charge to museum) beckons

Right: inside the Ars Nova Museum

next. The tower, peaking at 102m (335ft) above sea level, is the symbol of the city. The cathedal is both the mother church of the Lutheran Church of Finland, and the country's national shrine, and it celebrated its 700th anniversary in June 2000. The Bishop's See of the Diocese of Finland was transferred here in the 13th century as Turku gained in importance as a trading centre. By the end of that century a stone church had been erected and consecrated as the Cathedral Church of the Blessed Virgin Mary and St Henry – Henry was the first Bishop of Finland – in 1300. Additions were made over the ensuing centuries, and it wasn't until the end of the 15th century that it began to resemble

what we see today. However, the Great Fire of 1827 caused considerable damage and the present tower was added soon afterwards.

The interior also dates from restorations that were carried out after the fire, and is one of the finest examples of Finnish architecture. The walls and roof of the chancel are adorned with Romantic frescoes by R W Ekman, the court painter who is considered the father of Finnish painting. The frescoes depict scenes from the life of Christ and the two main events in the history of the Finnish Church – the baptism of the first Finnish Christians by Bishop Henry, and the presentation to King Gustav Vasa of the first Finnish translation of the New Testament by the Reformer Michael Agricola, whose statue stands outside in the gardens. A small museum is in the south gallery.

Turku Art Museum

Now cross back over the Aura River and make your way back through the modern city to the Market Square, from where you walk up Aurakatu to Puolalanpuisto Park. Here, on the top of the hill, a huge granite building with a rustic façade has undergone lengthy renovation to become, once again, the **Turku Art Museum** (Turun taidemuseo; tel: 262 7100; www.turuntaidemuseo.fi; Tues–Fri 11am–7pm, Sat and Sun 11am–5pm; admission charge). This palatial building was inaugurated as an art gallery in the spring of 1904 and during the five weeks of its first exhibition more than 8,000 people, out of a total city population of just 42,000, passed through the doors. From Puolalanpuisto Park, it is a short walk back to the station for the return to Helsinki.

Above and Right: the exterior of Turku Cathedral and one of its stained-glass windows

4. TALLINN, ESTONIA *(see map, p64)*

A visit to the capital of Estonia, its wonderfully preserved medieval heart now a UNESCO World Heritage Site. The attractions are truly remarkable, including a castle, cathedral, city walls and colourful old houses, and the atmosphere is quite different from that in Helsinki.

High-speed ferries to Tallinn take about 1½ hours, but the Gulf of Finland freezes in winter, so some services are seasonal. Flights are more expensive, but take just 18 minutes to cover the 85-km (53-mile) journey (see Practical Information, page 86). By making an early start you can see the most important sites in a day, but an overnight stay will allow for a more leisurely exploration.

Directly across the Gulf of Finland from Helsinki, Tallinn is the capital of the Republic of Estonia, a country on the eastern Baltic coast, bordering Russia and Latvia. The city has a fascinating and turbulent history. Ancient Estonians established a trading post here in the 10th century, and between 1219 and 1346 it was ruled by the Danes, who sold the northern Estonian territory to the German Teutonic Order and established the city as a member of the Hanseatic League of trading towns.

Estonia later aligned itself with the Swedes against the Russians and took an oath of allegiance to King Erik XIV in the summer of 1561, but after the Great Northern War, initiated by Tzar Peter I of Russia in 1700, the Russians took over and ruled until 1917, with Tallinn accorded a special autonomous status as a stronghold within the Russian state. After the Russian Revolution of 1917, on 24 February 1918, Estonia declared itself independent, but it wasn't until after the ensuing War of Independence that Tallinn became the capital of the Independent Republic of Estonia, on 2 February 1920. This period of independence lasted just 20 years, until Soviet forces occupied Estonia, established bases for the Red Army and Baltic Navy and abolished its independence.

On 28 August 1941 the Germans invaded, and later in World War II the Soviets attacked again, causing massive damage during an air raid on 9 March, 1944 and succeeding in finally ousting the Germans in September of that year. This did not prove beneficial for Estonia as the conquerors initiated reprisals on a wide scale. This uneasy period lasted until 20 August 1991, when the Supreme Soviet of Estonia re-established the country's independence, although the last Russian troops were not banished until 1994.

Despite these centuries of strife and turmoil, Tallinn's Old Town has sur-

Right: the fine view from Tallinn's St Olav's Church

vived relatively unscathed, and its status as a living medieval monument was recognised by UNESCO in 1997 when it added the Old Town to the World Heritage List. In May 2004 Estonia became a member of the EC.

Around Town Hall Square

As time will be of the essence on a day trip to Tallinn, it is a good idea to take a taxi from the ferry terminal (or the heliport) directly to **Town Hall Square** (Raekoja plats), the main place of interest in the Lower Town (All-linn). The square has been Tallinn's marketplace and social centre for more than seven centuries. Dominating the square is the **Town Hall** (Raekoja), whose **tower** has a viewing platform offering spectacular views (tel: 645 7900; mid-May–mid-Sept: admission charge). Although a previous structure was erected around 1342 this attractive building dates from the early 15th century, and is the oldest intact Gothic town hall in Northern Europe. The **Old Thomas** (Vana Toomas) weathervane at the top of the eight-sided tower was added in 1530.

The square is pleasing in its own right, with numerous interesting buildings, some of them pastel coloured. The old **Chemist Shop** (tel: 631 4860; Mon–Fri 9am–7pm, Sat 9am–5pm) was founded in 1422 and is thought to be one of the first of its kind in Europe. Naturally enough, there is no short-

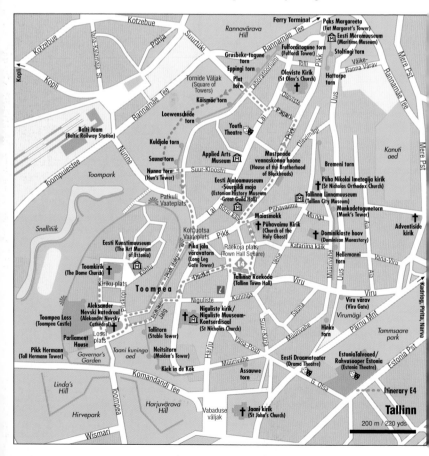

age of cafés and restaurants, and in the summer, when many of them have outside tables and chairs on raised platforms, this is an ideal place to soak up the ambience of this engaging city. You could also have lunch here before exploring more of the city. Try the **Balthasar**, Raekoja plats 11, which calls itself Estonia's first garlic restaurant, and even has ice cream with honey and garlic sauce. It's in the same ancient building as the chemist shop, with plenty of atmosphere and nice views over the square. Just off the square, at Dunkri 8, the **Kuldse Notsu Kõrts** (The Little Piggy Inn) is a country-style restaurant offering authentic Estonian cuisine, which includes pork dishes, crayfish, lots of potatoes and home-made black bread.

Church of the Holy Ghost

Among Tallinn's greatest attractions are its well-preserved city walls, but before admiring them go through Saiakang, just to the side of the chemist shop, and turn into Pühavaimu to the **Church of the Holy Ghost** (tel: 644 9911; Wed–Sun 10am–5pm; admission charge). This is easily identifiable by the attractive old clock on its façade – the oldest in Tallinn – to the left of the main doors. Dating from the 13th century, and built by the Order of the Holy Ghost, it is an Estonian Evangelical-Lutheran church that remained popular after the Reformation and from where the first sermons were given in the Estonian language. The interior is richly decorated, and includes Gothic wood sculptures and an altar dating from 1483 that is considered one of the four most precious medieval works of art in the country.

The church is almost on the corner of Pikk, a nice little street with an array of colourful stone houses, some of which were once guild houses. Particularly grand is the **House of the Brotherhood of Blackheads** (tel: 631 3199; www.mustpeademaja.ee; daily 10am–7pm). This brotherhood, for unmarried merchants, played an important role in the political life of medieval Tallinn. Most of the building is 16th century, including the Renaissance façade, while a splendid doorway dates from around 1640. It is a popular concert venue.

Right: Town Hall Square, Tallinn

At the junction with Pagari, where you should turn left, there is a formidable building with bricked-up basement windows. This was the headquarters of the NKVD – better known by its later name, the KGB. Here, perceived enemies of the Soviet Union were interrogated then shot or sent to Siberian work camps. A plaque recalls the thousands of Estonians who suffered here.

The City Walls and the Cathedral

At the end of Pagari go directly across into Suurtüki and then into the Square of Towers Park for the best views of the **City Walls** (Tallinna Linnaamüür), showing just how formidable these fortifications were. The walls encompassed 2.5km (1½miles), and about 75 percent still stand today. In the Middle Ages, there were six gates and no fewer than 66 towers, but now only 19 survive, and the ones in this stretch are oddly shaped and inconsistent in size, topped by irregular, conical, red-tiled roofs. Each of the towers has a name.

To inspect the parapets more closely, follow the walls around to the corner of Suur-Kloostri and Väike-Kloostri, and from there climb up the **Nun's Tower** (Nunna torn; tel: 644 9867; Jun–Aug Mon–Fri 11am–7pm, Sat–Sun 11am–4pm; Apr–May and Sept Tues–Fri noon–6pm, Sat–Sun 11am–4pm; winter hours vary; admission charge) and cross the wooden platform towards the Bath Tower and Golden Leg Tower *(Sauna and Kuldjala)*. From this perspective, you can see how the Upper Town (Toompea) dominates Tallinn.

Stroll along Väike-Kloostri then go through the rather run-down 14th-century gate with an elegant weathervane, and enter a long, steep street called Pikk jalg (Long Leg). Here you will see artists selling watercolours. At the top, on Castle Square (Lossi plats), **St Alexander Nevsky Cathedral** (tel: 644 3484; daily 9am–8pm; free) looms over the area, dominated by five unmistakable onion domes. Named in honour of the Russian duke who attacked southeastern Estonia in the first part of the 13th century, the cathedral was constructed between 1894 and 1900 on the orders of Tzar Alexander III. This massive Russian Orthodox church is an anomaly in Tallinn and of no real architectural or historical importance. Despite the period of Russian rule, most Estonians retain their Lutheran traditions, and many of this city's Gothic churches are more architecturally interesting than this extravaganza. The bell tower contains Tallinn's grandest collection of bells, the largest weighing 15 tonnes; the entire ensemble is played before each service.

excursions

Toompea Castle

Opposite the cathedral's main entrance is the pink baroque facade of **Toompea Castle**, with the city's coat of arms – three lions on a gold background – above the main arch. It derives from the royal coat of arms of Denmark, which ruled Estonia from the early 13th to mid-14th century. From this angle, Toompea doesn't look much like a castle, because the parts you see were rebuilt in the 18th century when it housed the provincial government. However, the first fortress on the site, built by the Danish monarch, Waldemar II, dates from the early 13th century. After Tallinn became the capital of a newly independent Estonia in 1920, a parliament (Riigikogu) was incorporated into the remains of a former convent in the south wing of the castle. The dominant feature of the building is the battlemented, 46m (151ft) 14th-century tower on the southwestern corner. Called **Pikk Hermann** (Tall Hermann), the traditional German name for a castle's main tower, it is the symbol of Tallinn. After a 50-year gap, the blue, black and white tricolour, the national flag of Estonia, was raised here once again in 1991.

One more church in the Upper Town merits a visit. Take Toom-Kooli – between the cathedral and the castle, passing an unusual sculpture of a man's head on one of the mansions – to the **Dome Church** (Toomkirk; summer Tues–Sun 9am–5pm; winter Tues–Sun 9am–3pm; free), dating from the time of the first Danish invaders in the 13th century, when it was just a wooden hall, dedicated to St Mary the Virgin. It is the oldest church on mainland Estonia, and the country's main Lutheran church. The Gothic exterior dates from the 14th century, when the church was rebuilt, while the interior was remodelled and a baroque spire added after the fire of 1684. It became the Baltic nobility's parish church, as is reflected by the wooden coats of arms on the walls.

The Danish King's Garden

Now, retrace your steps back to Castle Square and pass through the fortifications into the **Danish King's Garden** (Taani Kuninga aed), a little park inside the walls that overlooks the Lower Town. This is also home to two impressive towers – the **Kiek in de Kök** and **Neitsitorn** – and more fortified walls. In the far left-hand corner is a metal gateway leading to a cobbled alleyway; another gate leads through an archway to the left that takes you back to Pikk jalg (Long Leg). Directly in front, a set of steep steps is named Lühike jalg (Short Leg); this is the preferred route back to the Lower Town. At the bottom, take Rataskaevu, and pass the Hotel St Petersburg – the oldest continuously functioning hotel in Tallinn – into Dunkri and back to Town Hall Square where you can sit at one of th cafés and savour the atmosphere before finding a taxi to take you back to the ferry port (or heliport) for the return trip to Helsinki.

Left: St Alexander Nevsky Cathedral
Above: view of Tallinn from the Castle Tower

Leisure *Activities*

SHOPPING

The main shopping district in Helsinki fits neatly into a rectangular area between Central Railway Station, the Esplanadi, Mannerheimintie and Senate Square and Market Hall. The two largest department stores and a shopping centre *(see below)*, connected by a tunnel, are to the east along Mannerheimintie, near the station.

Along Aleksanterinkatu, and the smaller streets that cross it on a north–south axis, you will find everything from fashionable clothes boutiques to souvenir shops, as well as an eclectic array of restaurants, bars and nightclubs, and two shopping galleries with a wide range of goods. In the 19th century the city blocks were better known by names than by street addresses, and this idea has been revived for the five blocks on either side of Aleksanterinkatu, from Mannerheimintie to Senate Square. This is now affectionately known as the Zoo, as each block is named after and associated with a particular animal.

Local specialities include the beautiful Spectrolite jewellery, often set in silver, available at Kalevala Koru. Spectrolite is found only in the southeast corner of Finland. It is a feldspar stone that belongs to the Labradorite family, and glows magnificently with iridescent shades of green, dark blue and yellow.

The Marttiini shop near Senate Square specialises in knives of all kinds. There is a wide range of excellent goose- and duck-down products on show at Joutsen. They include slippers and travel pillows as well as duvets, and an innovative range of warm and fashionable coats and jackets.

Some attractive souvenirs, dolls, and leather and fur items are found on the stalls in Market Square. The nearby Old Market Hall has an exceptional selection of speciality delicatessen foods including such unusual delicacies as bear meat. The Herkku

Supermarket in the Stockmann department store *(see below)* is also a good place for local gourmet products.

Expect to find prices higher than in the UK, and in some instances substantially higher than in the USA.

Department Stores

Stockmann
Aleksanterinkatu 52B
Tel: 91 211
www.stockmann.fi
Mon–Fri 9am–9pm, Sat 9am–6pm
Opened in 1862, this is Finland's oldest and largest department store, seven floors high and covering a complete city block. It is perhaps a little on the expensive side, but full of high-quality merchandise and with an excellent souvenir department. Don't miss the Herkku Supermarket, which stocks an enticing selection of Finnish and exotic specialities; and the connected Academic Bookstore (Akateeminen), with four floors and thousands of books.

Sokos
Mannerheimintie 9
Tel: 010 7665100
www.sokos.fi
Mon–Fri 9am–9pm, Sat 9am–6pm
Located between Mannerheimintie and Central Railway Station, this smaller department store is in an emblematic building that was opened in 1952 in time for the Olympic Games. Prices are relatively high here, but quality is excellent. Sharing the same building is the Sokos hotel, a restaurant and a supermarket.

Left: shades of summer at an open-air café-bar on Cathedral Square
Right: in search of fun and freedom

Anttila
Kaivokatu 6/Salomonkatu 13
Tel: 1053 4500
www.anttila.fi
Mon–Fri 9am–9pm, Sat 9am–6pm
Opposite Central Railway Station, and connected to it by a tunnel, this shop started out as a mail-order company in the 1950s. It now competes with its two larger rivals by offering a good range of products at more affordable prices.

Shopping Centre

Forum
Mannerheimintie 20A
Tel: 565 7450
www.cityforum.fi
Mon–Fri 9am–9pm, Sat 9am–6pm (not all the shops have the same opening hours)
On the east side of Mannerheimintie, Forum is the largest shopping centre in the centre of Helsinki and incorporates 120 shops offering everything from fashion to electronics and groceries to gifts. On the lower level there is a food hall, including a choice of restaurants; the Fazer Café is particularly worth a visit. The Amos Anderson Art Museum *(see page 41)* is attached to the centre.

glass dome includes around 50 high-quality stores and boutiques, including Marimekko, Mexx, Bam Bam and Bang & Olufsen, as well as assorted cafés and restaurants.

Kiseleffin Basaari
Aleksanterinkatu 28
Mon–Fri 9am–5pm, Sat 9am–2pm
Occupying an historic building on the south side of Senate Square, this gallery is bursting with delightful little shops and kiosks offering an attractive selection that ranges from hand-crafted jewellery to unusual toys and craft-type souvenirs, as well as a shop selling all manner of things connected with saunas.

Factory Outlet

Arabia Centre
Hämeentie 135
Tel: 204 39 3507
www.arabia.fi
Mon–Fri 10am–8pm, Sat–Sun 10am–4pm
This is the largest outlet for Arabia ceramics, Iittala glass and Hackman ceramics and homeware, plus OPA and Pentik homeware shops. There are special discounts and mark-down prices. There is also a tax-free shopping and export service.

Guided tours of the factory are available on request (tel: 204 39 5326; e-mail: taina.gronqvist@ittala.com).

Shopping Galleries

Kämp Galleria
Kluuvikatu 4
www.kampgalleria.fi
Mon–Fri 10am–8pm, Sat 10am–5pm
Relatively new to the Helsinki shopping scene, this three-storey emporium with its impressive

Top: Finland's oldest department store. **Left:** the glass dome of Kämp Galleria

Speciality Shops

Kalevala Koru
Unioninkatu 25 and at the Airport Shop at Helsinki Airport
Tel: 207 611380
www.kalevalakoru.com

Owned by the Association of Women of the Kalevala, and formed in 1935, this is a fascinating jewellery store, between Senate Square and Market Square. Unusual and beautiful items of jewellery are produced, based on historical piecess. Look especially at those made from Spectrolite and set in silver *(see page 69)*. Also sells traditional outfits, woollen garments, shawls, hats, etc.

Kankurin Tupa
Pohjoisesplanadi 35. Tel: 626 182
Mannerheimintie 40. Tel: 492 535
Hotel Grand Marina. Tel: 650 031
www.kankurintupa.fi

These three locations have an amazing array of souvenirs, as well as the largest collection of hand-knitted garments in Finland – sweaters, hats, scarves and mittens. There are also knives, jewellery and silver from Lapland, crystal by Mats Jonasson, Christmas decorations and ceramics.

Joutsen
Museokatu 8
Tel: 448 126
www.joutsen.com

Joutsen, the northernmost manufacturer of down products in the world, uses only goose- and duck-down from the Arctic region – mainly Siberia – acquired as a by-product of the food industry. The water used to wash it has been filtered through glacial ridges. The products – from duvets and pillows to jackets and slippers – are light as well as warm, and the garments are attractive.

Marttiini
Aleksanterinkatu 28
Tel: 633 207
www.marttiini.fi
Mon–Fri 10am–6pm, Sat 10am–4pm

In a street next to Senate Square, Marttiini sells durable, traditional knives, which are often used for decoration, and sets of good-quality kitchen knives.

Schroder
Unioninkatu 23
Tel: 656 656

Between Senate Square and Market Square, this is a traditional shop for fishing and hunting. It has a huge section of fishing tackle, including one of the widest ranges of the esteemed Abu Garcia reels. There are also knives, from the Finnish Marttiini models to the renowned Swiss Victorinox; fine-quality waterproof clothing; Suunto wristop computers, and other gadgets for the modern hunter.

Sypressi
Unioninkatu 23 (between Senate Square and Market Square)
Tel: 625 645

The only store in Helsinki that stocks the well-known and attractive Oleana range of Norwegian sweaters, cardigans and other woollen garments, along with specially designed accessories such as jewellery and matching wristbands.

Markets

Helsinki's markets are worth a visit, even if you only want to browse, as they are full of colour and atmosphere. They can be found in Market Square and Old Market Hall around the South Harbour, at Hakaniemi Market Hall and open-air market and the Hietaniemi Antique and Art Centre and Flea Market. They are described more fully in the respective tours

Right: sunseekers on Market Square

EATING OUT

Helsinki has a wide selection of restaurants, ranging from several honoured with Michelin stars to small, cosy places serving wholesome, inexpensive meals. Menus often reflect seasonal produce. In summer, this includes new potatoes, fresh vegetables, salmon, whitefish and Baltic herring, as well as crayfish, which are in season from late-July until September. In the autumn, mushrooms and game begin appearing on menus,

and berries, such as cloudberries, blueberries and lingonberries, make delightful desserts. In the winter, the thick ice covering the lakes and rivers is broken, to find succulent fresh fish such as turbot, whitefish and other members of the salmon family.

Meal times are early compared to some European cities – usually 6.30am–10am for breakfast, 11am–1pm for lunch and 6.30–9pm for dinner. Inexpensive lunches (*loumas*) can be had at cafés (*kahvilas*).

Drinking

Medium-strength beer is available at most cafés, and a full range of beverages is sold at fully licensed restaurants and bars. Restaurants serve beer from 9am and other alcoholic drinks from 11am, but stop serving them half an hour before they close. The basic measures are 4cl (1.3fl oz) for spirits, 8cl (2.7fl oz) for fortified wines and 12cl (4fl oz) for table wines; beer is served either in 0.33-litre (0.7 pint) bottles or in 0.4-litre (0.8 pint) glasses. Not all restaurants are licensed, so check before you go. The minimum legal

age for drinking alcohol in restaurants is 18.

The most popular beer in Finland is Lapin Kulta (Lapland's Gold), brewed with water from the clear mountain streams in northern Lapland. It's usually 4.5 or 5.2 percent, but the special 7.0 percent brew will appeal to those with a taste for stronger beers. Wine, relatively expensive, is often drunk with meals, and you will find both local and imported vintages on offer.

Vodka is particularly popular in Finland and Finlandia is the country's best-selling brand, distilled with crystal-clear water that has been naturally filtered through deep moraine ridges. Berries grow everywhere and the Finns make them into tasty liqueurs.

Drinks are usually more expensive in Finland than in the UK or USA and many Finns cross the Gulf of Finland to buy it more cheaply in Tallinn, Estonia, particularly since that country joined the EC in 2004 and restrictions have been relaxed.

The Helsinki Menu

To promote Finnish cuisine and raise the prestige of local ingredients, a number of restaurants offer a special 'Helsinki Menu' consisting of three or more courses and featuring the best of Finnish seasonal produce. Participating restaurants display a blue oval sign with a four-pronged fork on it.

Price Guide

The price guide is for the average cost of a three-course meal without wine.
€€€ = over €50
€€ = €25 to 50
€ = below €25

Above: a food stall on Market Square
Right: time for tea

RESTAURANTS

Bellevue
Rahapajankatu 3
Tel: 179 560
www.restaurantbellevue.com
In the shadow of the Uspenski Orthodox Cathedral this is the oldest Russian restaurant in Helsinki, opened in 1917. The ambience is delightfully old-fashioned and the cuisine traditional – especially *blinis* at the beginning of Lent and at the Easter feasts. Try the pot-roast bear steak if the price doesn't deter you. €€€

Chez Dominique
Ludviginkatu 3–5
Tel: 612 7393
www.chezdominique.fi
Since opening in 1998, this Scandinavian gourmet restaurant has gone from strength to strength and Hans Välimäki, probably Finland's most famous chef, has now earned a second Michelin star. Close to the Esplanadi, and with seating for just 34, Chez Dominique is renowned for inventive cuisine such as seared fois gras with a white port and golden raisin sauce. €€€

G W Sundmans
Eteläranta 16
Tel: 622 6410
This esteemed restaurant, with one Michelin star, is next to Market Square, in a 19th-century Empire-style building designed by Engel. Although the building and decor are traditional, the cuisine is not: expect light, modern dishes using the best seasonal produce available. The extensive wine list includes some surprisingly inexpensive wines. €€€

George
Kalevankatu 17
Tel: 647 662
www.george.fi
This delightful little restaurant, which has a Michelin star, and specialises in international cuisine with a Scandinavian emphasis, using fresh produce. Choose from the Menu George, the Menu Vert or from the à la carte, which may feature such dishes as wild duck steak, red cabbage and roasted root vegeta-

bles, or tongue with goat's cheese potato purée and green pepper sauce. €€€

Havis Amanda
Eteläranta 16
Tel: 6869 5660
www.royalravintolat.com
Named after the nearby statue that is the symbol of Helsinki, this is the city's finest seafood restaurant. Opened in 1973, it offers Finnish fresh- and salt-water fish dishes and more exotic specimens from around the globe. €€€

Palace Gourmet
Eteläranta 10
Tel: 1345 6715
In the Palace Hotel, with fantastic views over the South Harbour, this has been a local favourite since 1952 and has a nostalgic 1950s ambience. The cuisine is Finnish/French, with international influences, and reflects the changing seasons. The wine cellar offers 400 vintages. Voted Restaurant of the Year in 2003. €€€

Kirja
Kirjatyöntekijänkatu 10
Tel: 135 5965
Kirja may be a little difficult to find as it is away from the main tourist area, but it is well worth the effort. It has been renowned

Top: autumn bounty

for its Finnish haute cuisine since 1935, and the traditional elegance of the dining room recalls that era. You will find such delicacies as duck liver with fig sauce and herb salad for a starter, followed by a fine selection of seafood, fish, fowl, venison and calf's liver for main courses. **€€–€€€**

Klippan Palace
Luoto
Tel: 633 408
The red roof of this distinguished wooden villa is easily recognised on the island of Luoto, in the South Harbour. Reached by ferry, it is a summer restaurant only open from May to September. There's a pleasant environment and a menu primarily based on Finnish ingredients, with one of the specialities being the excellent local crab. **€€–€€€**

Nokka
Kanavaranta 7
Tel: 687 7330
Located in one of the old red-brick buildings under the Orthodox Cathedral, this is a restaurant of great character with brick walls, wooden beams and an eclectic decor, featuring among other things old divers' helmets as light fittings. The menu features Arctic char, duck, lamb and snails, wild mushrooms, and wild berries for puddings. **€€–€€€**

Palace Ranta
Eteläranta 10
Tel: 134561
On the second floor of the Palace Hotel, this restaurant has panoramic views over the South Harbour. Both the design and the beautifully presented cuisine are contemporary. It has international visiting chefs two or three times a year, and makes an ideal stop for lunch or dinner. **€€–€€€**

Aino
Pohjoisesplanadi 21
Tel: 624 327
Opened in 2003, the Aino has a fine location by the Esplanadi and a relaxing atmosphere. The menu, which changes seasonally, includes Finnish fresh- and salt-water fish, lamb, reindeer, root vegetables, wild mushrooms and berries. Don't forget to try 'Aino's snaps', the restaurant's own version of schnapps, which is served in hand-made stoneware cups. **€€**

Café Carelia
Mannerheimintie 56
Tel: 2709 0976
www.carelia.info
This stylish, modern café/restaurant is conveniently close to the Opera House. It was originally a pharmacy, but has more recently become a restaurant, and great care has been taken to preserve the old character of the building. The cuisine is Mediterranean using fresh Finnish products, but the chef specialises in mussels, prepared in a variety of ways. **€€**

La Bodega
Yliopistonkatu 5
Tel: 278 1855
www.labodega.fi
This Spanish restaurant is part of a complex that also incorporates the Uniq nightclub and the Arctic Icebar, which maintains a temperature of -5°C (23°F) – warm clothes and gloves are provided for patrons. The restaurant menu is varied, with a small but interesting selection of tasty and authentic Spanish dishes, with recommended wines to match, and a special, set-price 'slow food' menu. **€€**

Ristorante Papà Giovanni
World Trade Centre (1st Floor)
Keskuskatu 7
Tel: 622 6010
Opened in 1996, the Papà Giovanni has a decidedly Italian atmosphere and decor, as well as Italian cuisine. The menu features most things you would expect to find in an Italian restaurant, including some appealing desserts, and the wine bar offers a cigar selection. **€€**

Left: terrace dining in summer

Lapland Restaurant
Annankatu 22
Tel: 645 550
www.lappires.com
A typical Lapland-style restaurant with an interior that is a re-creation of a traditional wooden summer house. The cuisine, too, is authentic. Starting with a Lappish aperitif, you might then try sirloin of reindeer with creamed juniper berry potatoes and game sauce, and round off your meal with delicious Lappish farm cheese in cinnamon cream. €€

Romanov
Yrjönkatu 15
Tel: 642 394
www.romanov.fi
Opened in 2003 in a beautiful 1896 neo-Renaissance mansion, this is the latest addition to Helsinki's array of Russian restaurants. Enter through a fine wrought-iron and glass gate to be delighted by the 19th-century classical decor, recreated here by one of the city's best-known interior designers. The interesting menu in two parts – one featuring classic dishes, the other offering new Russian cuisine, and two set menus are available. €€

Ravintola Lasipalatsi
Mannerheimintie 22–24
Tel: 7424 290
www.ravintola.lasipalatsi.fi
Located in the 'Glass Palace', between the railway station and the bus station, this restaurant has been renovated and now features a 1930s-style decor. The menu, like the seasons, changes four times a year and features typical Finnish ingredients such as fresh fish, local cheeses and full-flavoured wild berries. €–€€

Café Bar No 9
Uudenmaankatu 9
Tel: 621 4059
A few minutes' walk away from the Swedish Theatre, at the head of the Esplanadi, this little restaurant/bar has a trendy decor and it has become a popular hot-spot. The single-page menu offers a surprisingly wide variety of sandwiches, salads, soups, stir-fried dishes and pasta, at very economical prices. €

Palace Café
Eteläranta 10
Tel: 1345 6793
On the first floor of the Palace Hotel, with a terrace overlooking the South Harbour, this is one of the best value-for-money opportunities in Helsinki. Open from 7am–3pm Monday to Friday – although the kitchen closes at 2pm – it offers a salad, main course and coffee or dessert; or soup and a selection from the buffet, for under €8. There is also a daily, hot vegetarian dish. €

Satkar
Lönnrotinkatu 26
Tel: 611 077
Nepalese decor and style and delightful food, including Tandoori dishes, make this one of Helsinki's most popular 'ethnic' restaurants. €

Sir Eino Olutravintola
Eteläesplanadi 18
Tel: 856 85770
An English-Irish style pub with full-bodied beers and ciders and pub food, including meat grilled on an open fire. Live music. €

Spaghetteria
World Trade Centre (Ground Floor)
Tel: 6226 0111
A popular pasta bar that is part of the Papà Giovanni group, with a restaurant on the first floor and the lively Caffè Giovanni nearby. It offers good pastas, pizzas and salads, along with Italian wines, all at very reasonable prices and in a clean, modern setting. €

Right: food-to-go on Helsinki's Market Square

NIGHTLIFE

Helsinki has a wide variety of nightlife, ranging from cultural attractions such as orchestral concerts, opera, ballet and theatre, to international musicals and entertainers and evening sporting events – particularly hockey, the country's favourite sport – in the winter months.

There are many other theatres in Helsinki, in addition to those listed here, including an open-air stage at Suomenlinna during the summer. Details can be found at the Theatre Information Centre, tel: 135 7887; www.teatteri.org.

Those who like to chance their arm will find that the Grand Casino Helsinki, across from the railway station, not only offers a wide array of games and slot machines but is a complete entertainment complex, featuring restaurants as well as international variety shows and cabaret artists.

The nightclub and bar scene, mainly centred in the area close to Central Railway Station, is particularly vibrant and ranges from jazz clubs, sophisticated nightclubs and appealing bars – including a sauna bar – that, particularly at the weekend, will keep you going until the early hours of the morning.

The gay scene is also well catered for, and features the largest gay café, bar, disco and nightclub in the Nordic countries, and the only gay sauna in Finland *(see page 79)*.

Concert and Theatre Tickets
Tickets can be booked through the following organisations:

Lippupalvelu
Mannerheimintie 5
Tel: 600 10 800 (Local call charge plus €1 per minute)
www.lippupalvelu.fi

Lippupiste
Tel: 600 900 900 (Local call charge plus €0.95 per minute)
www.lippupiste.com

Tiketti
Forum, Third Floor
Yrjönkatu 29 C
Tel: 600 1 1616 (Local call charge plus 66 cents per minute)
www.tiketti.fi

International and Sporting Events
Hartwall Arena
Areenakuja 1
Tel: 204 1997
www.hartwall-areena.com
The first public event at this modern arena took place on 17 April 1997 with a Beach Boys concert, and that gives an idea of what you can expect on the bill here. Seating 13,665, and with its own dedicated railway station – the first stop from Central Railway

Above: Helsinki has a good mix of nightlife

Station, just a couple of minutes away – the eclectic selection of international events during the summer of 2004 included *Grease*, Cher's farewell tour, KORN, *Riverdance*, a Sarah Brightman concert, and ice hockey world cup games.

Culture

Music

Helsinki Philharmonic Orchestra
Finlandia Hall
Tel: 4024 265
www.hel.fi/filharmonia
The Helsinki Philharmonic was founded in 1882, and was the first professional symphony orchestra in the Nordic countries. From its foundation through to 1923 it presented the first performances of nearly all the symphonic works of Jean Sibelius, with the composer himself conducting. Today, the HPO, which has performed throughout Europe and in the USA and Japan, gives weekly concerts at the Finlandia Hall beween September and May.

Finnish Radio Symphony Orchestra
Tel: 1480 4336
www.yle.fi/rso
Performing principally at the Finlandia Hall, but also at the Hall of Culture, this fine orchestra plays an important role in Finnish music.

Chamber Music
Temppeliaukatu 3
Tel: 494 698
The Temppeliaukio (Rock) Church has amazing acoustics and concerts here, particularly those of Sibelius's work, are extremely popular.

Kulttuuritalo
Sturenkatu 4
Tel: 774 0270
www.kulttuuritalo.fi
Opened in 1958, this is architect Alvar Aalto's first public building in the Helsinki metropolitan area and was a product of his red-brick phase, as can clearly be seen from the exterior. The asymmetrical auditorium has some of the best acoustics in the country and has hosted performances by numerous Finnish classical, pop and rock musicians, as

well as the Finnish Broadcasting Company and Finnish Radio Symphony Orchestra. International groups such as Manhattan Transfer have also performed here.

Sibelius Academy of all Music
Pohjoinen Rautatiekatu 9
Tel: 0207 5390
www.siba.fi
The only music academy in Finland – named, not surprisingly, after the country's most famous composer – is also one of the largest in Europe, and it plays host to hundreds of classical concerts every year.

Opera and Ballet

Finnish National Opera
Helsinginkatu 58
Tel: 4030 2211
www.operafin.fi
The national opera company's programme forms an interesting mixture, with performances not only of pure classical works but also modern productions and a good selection of works that will appeal to a younger audience.

Theatre

Finnish National Theatre
Läntinen teatterikuja 1
Tel: 1733 1331
www.kansallisteatteri.fi
This is the oldest Finnish-language professional theatre company in the country, and one that has played an important cul-

Left: propping up a bar

from 7pm. There's a Piano Bar Mon–Fri 6–9pm and a spicy Cajun-Creole menu.

Umo Jazz House
Pursimiehenkatu 6
Tel: 6122 1914
http://umo.fi
The famous Umo Jazz Orchestra performs every Friday, and the Jazz Club show time is 9pm every evening, when you can hear all kinds of jazz by the best Finnish and international artists.

Nightclubs
Helsinki Club
Yliopistonkatu 8
Tel: 43 320
Found in the Hotel Helsinki, the club has three sections with different decor, and caters for varying ages, but most of its customers are fairly affluent.

10th Floor
Kaivokatu 3A
Tel: 1311 8223
An elite nightclub in a penthouse location, with a minimum entry age of 24 and smart dress code.

La Tour Club Premier
Mannerheimintie 5
Tel: 684 0740
Located in the New Student Union Building, across from the Stockmann store, this venue usually plays hits from the 1970s and 1980s and caters to a slightly older crowd.

Bars with a Difference
Ateljee Bar
Sokos Torni Hotel
Kalevankatu 26
Tel: 43 360
Designed by Aalto, and situated on the 12th floor, this chic bar not only has interesting drinks and a good cigar selection, but is also the highest point in central Helsinki, with spectacular views that extend over the city and beyond.

Saunabar
Eerikinkatu 27
Tel: 586 5550
This attractive bar also provides separate

tural role in Helsinki for more than 130 years. The theatre building has recently been restored.

The Swedish Theatre
Pohjoisesplanadi 2
Tel: 6162 1411
www.svenskateatern.fi
Within this baroque theatre, Swedish-language productions are performed.

Varied Events
Kaapelitehdas (Cable Factory)
Taliberginkatu 1C 15
Tel: 4763 8330
www.kaapelitehdas.fi
This ex-Nokia factory, now a cultural centre, is yet another venue in Helsinki where you can find a wide array of theatre, music and dance events.

Film
The Finnish Film Archive
Pursimiehenkatu 29–31
Tel: 615 400
www.sea.fi
A membership fee of €3.50 covers a ticket to performances that usually include classic and cult films. The Helsinki Film Festival, tel: 6843 5230; www.hiff.fi, is held every September.

Jazz Clubs
Happy Jazz Club Storyville
Museokatu 8
Tel: 408 007
www.storyville.fi
Close to the parliament building, and located in an old coal cellar, this is one of the most popular nightspots in Helsinki and has live, traditional jazz Mon–Sat from 10pm and Sun

Above: the Swedish Theatre
Right: outdoor performance

saunas for men and women, with a pool (book ahead except on Sun–Mon; towels available). There's also snooker, an Internet-lift (actually a non-functioning lift that's fitted out with Internet connection) and a DJ five nights a week playing mostly mellow sounds. There's occasional live music, too.

The Gay Scene

Bar Stuff

Eerikinkatu 14
Tel: 608 826
www.conhombres.fi
This is the oldest, and some say the best, gay bar in Helsinki, with a lively Latin-American theme. Open 4pm–2am.

Room

Erottaja 5
Tel: 622 70440
www.roombar.fi
This hot, sophisticated gay pub has a lounge-bar ambience. Open Mon–Thur 2pm–2am, Sat–Sun 2pm–3am.

DTM

Iso Roobertinkatu 28
www.dtm.fi
This claims to the largest gay café, bar, disco and nightclub in the Nordic countries. Nightclub open 10pm–4am.

Vogue

Sturenkatu 27A
Tel: 737 280
www.conhombres.fi/vogue.html
The only gay sauna in Finland. It has a swimming pool, bar and top-floor roof terrace. Open Sun–Thur 3–11pm, Fri–Sat 3pm–2am.

Gambling

Grand Casino Helsinki

Mikonkatu 19
Tel: 680 800
www.grandcasino.fi
Opened in 2004, this is one of the most modern casino's in Europe, designed by a Las Vegas architect, with 32 gaming tables offering the usual live games and some speciality tables. There are also 300 slot machines, restaurants, bars, international concerts and cabaret shows. Daily admission, upon presentation of a passport and being photographed for identification purpose, is €2; minimum entry age is 18; the dress code does not permit sports wear and the games are in cash (euros) only.

CALENDAR OF EVENTS

January

Throughout January – Disney On Ice. At the Hartwell Arena, Helsinki, www.hartwall-areena.com.
Throughout January – Fashion Fair. The biggest fashion fair in Finland, Helsinki, www.finnexpo.fi.
Throughout January – Antique and Design Fair. Held at the Cable Factory, Helsinki.

February

17 February – Parade of Graduating Students. Held along the Esplanadi and other streets, Helsinki.
Early to mid-February – Boat and Boating Fair, Helsinki, www.finnexpo.fi.
Mid-February – Student Jazz Festival, Tallinn, www.tudengijazz.ee.
Late February/early March – Musica Nova. Concerts of modern music at various locations, Helsinki.

March/April

15 March – Red Bull Snowboard Event. More than 30,000 people watch this event at Market Square, Helsinki.
Mid-March – Wine Expo. The largest wine fair in Finland, Helsinki, www.finnexpo.fi.
Late March/early April – Helsinki Beer Festival. Held at the Cable Factory, Helsinki. **Easter Saturday – Via Crucis**. Passion play at Senate Square, Helsinki.
Easter Saturday – Easter Bonfires, at Seurasaari, Helsinki.

April

April Jazz Espo. Helsinki's largest jazz happening, celebrating its 19th anniversary in 2005, tel: 455 0003; www.apriljazz.fi.
Late April – Jazzkaar. Annual international jazz festival with world-class performers, Tallinn, www.jazzkaar.ee.
23/24 April – St George's Day Fair, Tallinn.
30 April – *Havis Amanda* statue receives her graduate hat from students, Helsinki.

May

1 May – May Day. Traditional student celebrations, including a picnic at Kaivopuisto, Helsinki.

June

4–6 June – Old Town Days, Tallinn.
Early June to late August – Organ Night and Aria Festival. Every Thursday night at the Church of Espoo.
12 June – Helsinki Day. Celebrating the city's birthday in 1550. There are numerous events throughout the city, notably the traditional handicrafts market at Esplanadi and live music on the Esplanadi stage, Helsinki, www.hel.fi/helsinkipaiva.

Above: boat race on the Kaisaniemenlahti

Mid-June – Visit Finland's Provinces. Get to know one of Finland's provinces without going any further than Senate Square, Helsinki, www.hel.fi/maakuntajuhlat.

Third weekend in June – Midsummer celebrations. The largest family event in Finland includes a wedding (an engaged couple is chosen to participate), bonfires and other things, Seurasaari Island, Helsinki, www.kolumbus.fi/seurasaarisaatio.

End June to late July – Jazz Espa. Jazz concerts on the Esplanadi, Helsinki.

July

Early July – All Estonian Song and Dance Festival, Tallinn, www.laulupidu.ee.

Early July – Medieval Market. In the Old Town, Tallinn, www.folkart.ee.

Late July – Koneisto Festival of Electronic Music. Electronic music festival at the Cable Factory, Helsinki, tel: 600 10 800; www.koneisto.com.

August

Early August–International Organ Festival. The world's top organists participate, Tallinn, www.concert.ee.

Early to mid-August – International Association Athletics Federation (IAAF) 10th Annual Championships. To be held in Helsinki in 2005; the main venue will be the Olympic Stadium.

Mid-August – Finnish Fireworks Championships. At South Harbour, Helsinki.

Late August/September – Helsinki Festival. Music, theatre, dance, art and film events, with performers from Finland and abroad. www.helsinkifestival.fi.

End August – Espoo Cinè Film Festival. An international film festival at the Espoo Cultural Centre, www.espoocine.org.

September

Late September – Helsinki Salsa Festival. Held in a special tent at Central Railway Station.

Late September – Credo, International Festival of Sacred Music. Traditional and modern Orthodox music, Tallinn.

October

Early October – Herring Market. Fishermen sell herring and other fish, and also traditional dark bread to go with it, at Market Square, Helsinki, in Finland's oldest traditional event.

Mid-October – Choral Espoo Festival. A festival of international choral music, www.choralespoo.fi.

November

Mid-November – St Martin's Day Fair, Tallinn, www.folkart.ee.

Mid-November to early January – Winter Circus. A popular circus performed by the Dance Theatre Hurjaruuth, Helsinki, tel: 565 7250; www.hurjaruuth.fi.

Late November to mid-December – Tallinn Black Nights Film Festival, www.poff.ee.

Late November to January – Forces of Light. Organised for the 11th time in 2005. Primarily centred along the Esplanadi and in the Old Church Park, light and fire are used to create art and life during the darkest period of the year, Helsinki, www.hel.fi/valonvoimat.

December

Throughout December – Christmas Market. Traditional Estonian products and food and drink, Tallinn

Early to mid-Dec – Christmas Jazz. Estonian and international artists perform in various city locations, Tallinn. www.jazzkaar.ee.

6 December–Finnish Independence Day celebrations.

Early to mid-December – St Thomas Christmas Market. More than 120 booths selling all kinds of Christmas treats, gifts and handicrafts line the Esplanadi park, Helsinki.

31 December – New Year's Eve celebrations. Featuring speeches, concerts and fireworks in Senate Square, Helsinki.

Right: Esplanade Park is a popular venue for all kinds of celebrations

Practical Information

GETTING THERE

By Air
From the UK and Republic of Ireland
Finnair, www.finnair.com, works in co-operation with British Airways and has up to four flights a day using its own planes and up to three flights a day using BA planes, from London Heathrow to Helsinki; and up to two flights a day from Manchester – either direct or with a stop in Stockholm.

Finnair also operates non-stop flights between Dublin and Helsinki, except in the winter season, on Monday, Thursday, Friday and Sunday, with extra flights added in July on Tuesday and Wednesday.

Duo, www.duo.com, operates non-stop flights Sunday to Friday between Birmingham and Helsinki.

From North America
Finnair, www.finnair.com, operates a daily, year-round, non-stop service between New York City and Helsinki, and daily non-stop flights in the summer between Toronto, Canada and Helsinki.

American Airlines, www.aa.com, with a Finnair code-share, operates a daily service between New York City and Helsinki.

Icelandair, www.icelandair.com, operates flights during the summer from New York, Baltimore, Boston, Minneapolis and Orlando to Reykjavik with onward connections to Helsinki. At other times of the year, the connecting flight to Helsinki is by the Swedish airline, SAS.

Helsinki-Vantaa Airport, a modern facility with an excellent range of services is located about 20km (12 miles) north of Helsinki city centre, and the Finnair airport bus (currently €4.90) takes about 30 minutes to the Finnair City Terminal next to Central Railway Station. Taxis also take around 30 minutes to reach the city centre and cost in the region of €30.

TRAVEL ESSENTIALS

When to Visit
Because the weather is extremely cold and the days very short in winter, the best time to visit is between late April and late September. However, at either end of this period the weather can still be cold and damp, and it has been known to snow in mid-May.

Passports and Visas
Citizens of the Scandinavian countries – Denmark, Iceland, Norway and Sweden – do not need a passport to enter Finland. European Union nationals and citizens of Liechtenstein, Monaco, San Marino and Switzerland can enter Finland with either a valid passport or a valid ID card. Citizens of Australia, Canada, New Zealand, USA and certain other countries do not need a visa.

Vaccinations
No vaccinations are necessary.

Weather
Finland's climate is one of cold winters (in Jan–Feb it can drop to -20C /-4°F) and warm summers, when temperatures in Helsinki can rise to 30°C (86°F).

Clothing
Although July and August can be pleasantly warm, it's best to plan for all eventualities. The Finns layer their clothes, so they can be taken off or put on to suit the temperature. Sturdy walking shoes are advisable, especially as many of the city streets and pavements are cobbled.

Left: ready to depart, Central Railway Station
Right: here to help

GETTING ACQUAINTED

Electricity
The electric current in Finland is 220/230V, 50Hz, and adapters and transformers are available in airport shops.

Time Differences
Finland is two hours ahead of Greenwich Mean Time (GMT), and the difference between Eastern Standard Time (USA) and Finnish Standard Time is 7 hours. The 24-hour clock is used in Finland.

Geography
Finland is situated in northern Europe between the 60th and 70th parallels of latitude. Its neighbours are Sweden, Norway and Russia, with whom it shares land borders (the 1,269km/789 miles it shares with Russia mark the eastern border of the European Union), and Estonia to the south across the Gulf of Finland.

Finland is Europe's largest archipelago. It has an area of 338,000 sq. km (130,500 sq. miles), of which about a quarter is north of the Arctic Circle. It is about 69 percent forest and 10 percent water, with 187,888 lakes, 5,100 rapids and 179,584 islands.

Government
Finland has been an independent republic since 6 December 1917. The head of state is the president, who is chosen by direct popular vote, with a run-off between the two leading candidates after the first round of voting. The president may serve a maximum of two consecutive six-year terms. Parliament (Eduskunta) consists of one chamber with 200 members who are elected by direct popular vote, under a system of proportional representation, for a four-year term.

In the elections of 16 March 2003, nine parties were represented in parliament, the two largest being the Centre Party with 55 seats and the Social Democratic Party with 53 seats. They and the Swedish People's Party, with 8 seats, govern as a coalition.

Religion
Christianity reached Finland approximately 1,000 years ago, almost simultaneously from the east and west. Consequently, both the Evangelical Lutheran Church and the Orthodox Church are recognised as official religions, with about 85.7 percent affiliated to the former, 1 percent to the latter and 13.3 percent unaffiliated.

The first Sunday morning services in Finnish or Swedish are usually held at 10am. There are English-language services at 10am at the Merirasti Chapel, Jaluspolku 3, Meri-Rastila (Vuosaari) Helsinki, and at 2pm at the Temppeliaukio (Rock) Church, Lutherinkatu 3, Helsinki.

Roman Catholic services are held at St Henry's Cathedral, Phyän Henrikin aukio 1, tel: 682 4040, with Sunday Masses at 9.45am, 11am and 6pm; Tuesday and Thursday at 7.30am and Monday, Wednesday, Friday and Saturday at 6pm.

Anglican Episcopal services are held at the Anglian Church, Ruoholahden Kappeli chapel, Selkämerenkuja 1, tel: 680 1515, in English on Sunday at 10am.

Jewish services in Hebrew are held at the Synagogue, Malminkatu 26, tel: 5860 3121, on Saturday at 9am.

Population
Finland has a population of about 5.2 million people, of whom 67 percent live in urban areas and 33 percent in rural areas. Helsinki has a population of 560,000 (1,000,000 in the metropolitan area); Tampere's population is 199,000 and Turku's 182,000.

MONEY MATTERS

Currency
The Finnish currency is the euro (€), which consists of 100 cents. Bank notes are in denominations of 5, 10, 20, 50, 100, 200 and 500 and there are 5, 10, 20 and 50 cent coins as well as €1 and €2 coins.

Left: a wedding party poses

The currency in **Estonia** is the Estonian kroon (EEK), divided into 100 cents. Notes are in denominations of 1, 2, 5, 10, 25, 50, 100 and 500 EEK, plus 1 and 5 EEK coins. It is pegged at 15.65 EEK to the euro (€).

Credit Cards
American Express, Diner's Club, Eurocard, Access, MasterCard and Visa are accepted in hotels, restaurants and most shops.

Cash Machines
These are common, and are often identified by the OTTO sign.

Tipping
Generally, tipping is not expected – although recognition of good service from waiters, etc, by a tip of around 10–15 percent, is common practice and much appreciated.

Tax-Free Shopping
Anyone resident outside the EU and Norway can shop tax-free in Finland, saving 12–16 percent on purchases worth more than €40. Stores showing the tax-free shopping sign will issue customers with a cheque for the VAT refund amount that can be cashed on leaving the final EU country visited. Further information can be obtained from Global Refund Finland Oy, PO Box 460, 00101 Helsinki, tel: 6132 9600, www.globalrefund.com.

GETTING AROUND

Taxis
All taxis have a yellow *Taksi/Taxi* sign, which, when illuminated, indicates the taxi is vacant. Taxis can be ordered by phone (tel: 0100 0700 or 0100 0600), hailed in the street or found at a taxi rank. The basic fare (2004 rates) is €4.15, with the increments per kilometre, depending on the number of passengers. This fare rises to €6.40 Monday to Friday 8pm–6am and on Saturday and Sunday 4pm–6am.

Trams, Buses and Metro
Public transport in Helsinki is operated by **Helsinki City Transport (HKL)**, www.hel.fi/hkl, who have a variety of ticket schemes. Individual tram tickets can be bought from the driver for €1.80 or prepaid at ticket machines for €1.50. For the other forms of transport tickets cost €2 (individual) and €1.80 (prepaid). Tourist tickets for all forms of transport cost €5.40 for one day, €10.80 for three days and €16.20 for five days. All forms of transport are free for holders of the Helsinki Card *(see page 86)*. Although there is a Metro system, it is rather limited and is probably best used by visitors only to get to/from the Cable Factory.

Tram Tours
Trams are omnipresent in Helsinki, and it is almost a requirement for visitors to take one to get around town and enjoy more than they might otherwise see. Hop on a No 3T tram at any stop and you will find that it traces a figure-of-eight course around the centre of Helsinki in roughly one hour. The fare is €2 on board or €1.70 prepaid from a machine, and there is an interesting brochure on board detailing the sights and stops along the route.

Visitors may find the comforts offered by the **Spårakoff** more attractive. This is a tram coach converted into a pub, and from its bar you can enjoy refreshments while taking a 60-minute tour of Helsinki's main sights. Running between mid-May and early August, the tours start at Railway Square from Tuesday to Saturday at 2pm, 3pm, 5pm, 6pm, 7pm and in July also at 8pm, but you can hop on and off at any of the stops.

Above: trams are one of the best ways of getting around Helsinki

Audio City Tour, arranged by Helsinki Expert, tel: 2288 1200, www.helsinkiexpert.fi, departs from the Esplanadi Park/Fabianinkatu, and lasts 90 minutes, with sound effects and commentary in 11 languages, taking in all the most important and interesting sights in Helsinki. It runs in winter daily at 11am, in spring and autumn daily 11am and 1pm, in summer daily at 10am, 11am, noon, 1pm and 2pm (€20).

City-bike

Bicycles are a practical way of getting around Helsinki in summer, and there are 26 stands in the city centre where you can rent a bike by paying a deposit of €2. When you have finished with the bike, simply

return it to any City-bike stand and retrieve your €2 deposit.

Ferries to Suomenlinna

Ferries to Suomenlinna fortress leave regularly from Market Square. The journey takes about 15 minutes.

To Porvoo

There are frequent bus services to and from Porvoo, departing from the bus station in Helsinki and the market square in Porvoo, and the journey time, depending upon traffic, is around an hour. If you prefer to go by boat, the **Royal Line Shipping Company**, tel: (09) 612 2950, www.royalline.fi, operates the m/s *King* from Helsinki Market Square at 10am (late June–mid-Aug) and departs Porvoo for Helsinki at 3pm; the journey time is 3 hours.

On Wednesday, Friday and Saturday (plus Sunday in midsummer; check for details of other seasonal dates) the *J. L. Runeberg,* tel: 524 3331, www.msjlruneberg.fi, sets sail from Helsinki at 10am and returns from Porvoo at 4pm: journey time is 3 hours 20 minutes (€29).

To Tallinn, Estonia

There are several options for high-speed ferries that take about 1½ hours. The **Silja Line**, Helsinki, tel: 18 041, www.silja.fi; Tallinn, tel: 611 6611, operates the largest SuperSeaCats fast ferries. The Gulf of Finland freezes in winter, so some of these services are seasonal.

By air, **Copterline**, Helsinki Airport, tel: 358 9 6811/670, Hernesaari, Hernematalankatu 2, or Tallinn Heliport, tel: 610 1818, www.copterline.com, offers a fast if expensive way to cover the 85km (53 miles) between Helsinki and Tallinn; flight time is 18 minutes.

Helsinki Card

The **Helsinki Card** allows free admission to almost 50 museums, free travel on public transport in Helsinki, free travel on the ferry/waterbus to Suomenlinna and Korkeasaari, a free, guided city walk and reductions on other guided tours, a guide book with maps in four languages and discounts in some stores and restaurants. It can be purchased from the tourist office, from many hotels and other places, and costs (2004 rates) €25 for one day, €35 for two days and €45 for three days, with children's prices €10, €13 and €16, respectively.

HOURS AND HOLIDAYS

Business Hours

Banks are open Monday to Friday 9am–4.30pm.
Foreign Exchange points at Helsinki-Vantaa Airport in the Nordea arrival hall open Monday to Saturday 6am–5pm; and in Sampo arrival hall, Monday to Friday 3am–11pm, Saturday and Sunday 7am–11pm. **Stockmann** department store also has exchange points, as do the **Katajanokka Ferry Terminal**, Monday to Saturday 10am–noon, 3.45–8.45pm and Sunday 3.45–8.45pm, and the **Olympia Ferry**

Above: passing traffic, Suomenlinna Island

Terminal, daily 9.30–11am, 3–4.45pm.
Forex has exchange offices at Central Railway Station, tel: 669 001, Monday to Friday 8am–9pm, Saturday and Sunday 8am–9pm; Mannerheimintie 10, tel: 647 008, Monday to Friday 9am–7pm, Saturday 9am–3pm; Pohjoisesplanadi 27, tel: 636 256, Monday to Friday 9am–7pm, Saturday 9am–3pm; and at Asematunneli, tel: 621 3470, Monday to Friday 10am–6pm.

Post Offices are generally open Monday to Friday 9am–4.30pm.

Shops are usually open Monday to Friday 9am–5pm, Saturday 9am–3pm. Some of the bigger department stores stay open until 8pm Monday to Friday and until 4pm on Saturday. Most stores are closed on Sunday, except for those under the Helsinki Railway Station and some on the Esplanadi.

Public Holidays

Fixed dates:
1 January – New Year's Day (Uudenvuoden päivä)
6 January – Twelfth Day (Loppiainen)
1 May – May Day (Vapunpäivä)
24 December – Christmas Eve (Jouluaatto)
25 December – Christmas Day (Joulupäivä)
26 December – Boxing Day (Tapaninpäiv)

Moveable dates:
Late March/April – Good Friday (Pitkäperjantai)
Late March/April – Easter (Pääsiäinen)
Late May – Ascension Day (Helatorstai)
End May/June – Whitsun (Helluntai)
Late June – Midsummer's Day (Juhannus)
Early November – All Saints' (Day Pyhäinpäivä)

ACCOMMODATION

Hotels in Finland have a well-deserved reputation for cleanliness, a wide range of facilities, good service and comfortable, albeit rather small, rooms, regardless of their price category. However, the vast majority of hotels would be considered in the three- or four-star class, if there were a standardised rating system, so they are fairly expensive.

Most of the hotels in Helsinki are in the centre of town in an almost rectangular area between Central Railway Station in the north, the Esplanadi in the south, Mannerheimintie to the east and Senate Square and Market Hall to the west. There are a couple of larger ones (including the Scandic Hotel Continental) just to the north of this area, along Mannerheimintie, overlooking Hesperia Park and Töölönlahti Bay, while in an interesting area just across the Long Bridge, by the Hakaniemi Indoor and Outdoor Market, there is the excellent Hilton Helsinki Strand and a couple of smaller hotels.

The **Hotel Booking Center** (tel: 2288 1400, fax: 2288 1499, e-mail: hotel@helsinkiexpert.fi, www.helsinkiexpert.fi) is in the west wing of the railway station and is open June to August Monday to Friday 9am–7pm, Saturday 9am–6pm and Sunday 10am–6pm; September to May Monday to Friday 9am–6pm, Saturday 9am–5pm.

Price Guide
Approximate prices for a double room in high season.
€€€€ = Over €250
€€€ = €150–250
€€ = €50–150
€ = Under €50

Hotel Kämp
Pohjoisesplanadi 29
Tel: 576 111
Fax: 576 1122
www.hotelkamp.fi
This is Finland's most prestigious hotel. Dating from 1887, it has been completely renovated, retaining the ambience of that era but incorporating all the modern facilities that discerning travellers expect. Rooms are spacious and sumptuously decorated and appointed. There is a gourmet restaurant and a comfortable, relaxing bar. The Balance Club has the latest fitness equipment, along with steam showers, heated ceramic divans and sauna suites. €€€€

Hilton Helsinki Strand
John Stenbergin ranta 4
Tel: 39 351
Fax: 39 35 3255
www.helsinki-strand.hilton.com
Just across the Pitkäsilta Bridge from the Botanic Gardens, this is Helsinki's newest luxury hotel. It features an impressive

atrium with glass lifts, and offers a choice of 192 spacious rooms, which incorporate seven suites, two rooms for people with disabilities and 76 no-smoking rooms. There are two restaurants, a sauna suite, fitness room, 24-hour room service and a heated garage. The service is exemplary. €€€€

Hilton Helsinki Kalastajatorppa
Kalastajatorpantie 1
Tel: 45 811
www.hilton.com
Situated by the sea, surrounded by a verdant park and just 20 minutes or so from the city centre, this well-known hotel has 238 comfortable rooms, each with a sea or park view. The Oceana Restaurant serves a full breakfast, and the Meritorppa Restaurant has seafood specialities. There's also a fitness room, jogging and walking tracks and a tennis court. €€€€

Holiday Inn Helsinki City Centre
Elielinaukio 5
Tel: 5425 5000
Fax: 5425 5299
www.hi-helsinkicity.com
Opened for the 2003 summer season, and located next to the Central Railway Station, this hotel has 174 air-conditioned, non-smoking rooms. Facilities include a restaurant, lobby bar, business corner, mini-gym and two saunas. €€€€

Palace Hotel
Eteläranta 10
Tel: 1345 6660
Fax: 654 786
www.palacekamp.fi
This small hotel, with just 39 rooms (of which six are suites), has a fabulous location – the best in Helsinki – right next to the Market Square. Front-facing rooms have terraces with stunning views over the South Harbour and the two cathedrals. Built for the 1952 Olympic Games, it retains some of that ambience and style, and is rightly renowned for its selection of restaurants and its rooftop bar and terrace with an open barbecue. It also offers wood-fired and electric saunas, 24-hour room service and a good business centre. €€€€

Scandic Continental Helsinki
Mannerheimintie 46
Tel: 47 371
Fax: 47 37 2211
www.scandic-hotels.com
Directly across from the Töölö park, the Scandic has 512 pleasant rooms and 12 suites, and 170 have recently been refurbished. Try to get a room that's away from

the main road and, preferably, in Ambassador Class, which entitles you to use of the exclusive Ambassador Lounge. The hotel also has a restaurant, a cocktail bar, a coffee shop, a gift shop, a business centre, and the splendid Imperial Health Club with its pool, gymnasium and Turkish sauna. €€€–€€€€

Scandic Hotel Simonkenttä
Simonkatu 9
Tel: 683 80
Fax: 683 8111
www.scandic-hotels.com/simonkentta
This is an elegant hotel with modern architecture and ecological design, and it has fine views over the city centre. There are 359 rooms, including three suites and five rooms with access and facilities for disabled travellers. The restaurant features international and Scandinavian cuisine, and there's a rooftop pavilion, three saunas and a gymnasium. €€€–€€€€

Right: terrace of the Grand Marina

Sokos Hotel Torni
Yrjönkatu 26
Tel: 1234 604
Fax: 43 36 7100
www.sokoshotels.fi
Helsinki's only skyscraper hotel opened in 1931 and has rooms in both its Art Deco and *Jugendstil* buildings. Of the 154 rooms, 85 are non-smoking. There are restaurants and bars include the Ateljee *(see pages 41 and 78)*, with panoramic views; the American Bar, an international cocktail bar; and O'Malley's, the city's oldest Irish bar. There are also four saunas. **€€€–€€€€**

Radisson SAS Plaza Hotel
Mikonkatu 23
Tel: 77 590
Fax: 77 59 7100
www.radissonsas.com
Next to Central Railway Station and the Finnish National Theatre, this hotel occupies a building dating from 1917 that has been renovated to include up-to-date facilities. The 301 rooms include six suites and six rooms for people with disabilities. There's a restaurant, the Glass Bar, plus a sauna and gym. **€€€**

Radisson SAS Seaside Hotel
Ruoholahdenranta 3
Tel: 1234 707
Fax: 693 2123
www.radissinsas.com
Near the bottom of Bulevardi and Hietalahti Market, the Raddisson, renovated in 2003, has pleasing views over the western harbour and offers 364 modern, comfortable rooms of which 13 are suites. The hotel has a rooftop restaurant and bar, a summer terrace, and a sauna on the roof level, with fine views. **€€€**

Scandic Hotel Grand Marina Helsinki
Katajanokanlaituri 6
Tel: 16 661
Fax: 664 764
www.scandic-hotels.com/grandmarina
Just around the corner from Market Square, in a restored warehouse from the early 1900s and overlooking the harbour, this hotel has 462 rooms, including 20 suites and eight rooms for guests with disabilities, as well as rooms for non-smokers and people with allergies; all have recently been refurbished. It also has a restaurant, a lobby bar, three saunas, a gym and solarium, shops, hair salon and a business corner. **€€€**

Sokos Hotel Klaus Kurki
Bulevardi 2–4
Tel: 43 340
Fax: 43 34 7100
www.sokoshotels.fi
This is a medium-sized, comfortable hotel in a central location close to the antiques shops, boutiques and galleries of the Punavuori district. It has 136 rooms, of which 86 are non-smoking; a restaurant and a club featuring live music and, of course, a sauna. **€€€**

Hotelli Seurahuone
Kaivokatu 12
Tel: 69 141
Fax: 69 14 010
www.hotelliseurahuone.fi
This is one of Helsinki's most emblematic hotels. Opened in 1833, it was moved to its present position opposite Central Railway Station in 1914 and well-preserved *Jugendstil* features give it a singular atmosphere. There are 118 rooms and five suites, mostly non-smoking. It also has a bistro, bar and saunas. **€€€**

Hotel Anna
Annankatu 1
Tel: 616 621
Fax: 602 664
www.hotelanna.com
This is a small, comfortable hotel in an interesting part of Helsinki. The building dates from 1926, but the hotel was established in 1985, with extensive renovations undertaken in 1999. It has 64 rooms including three junior suites, all with TV, telephone, radio and mini-bar; about half are non-smoking and some are for guests with allergies. **€€€**

Hotel Rivoli Jardin
Kasarmikatu 40
Tel: 681 500
Fax: 656 988
www.rivoli.fi
In a townhouse right in the heart of the business and shopping area, this hotel has 55

rooms with one suite and one room for people with disabilities, a lobby bar and breakfast room, business centre and sauna. €€€

Scandic Gateway Helsinki Airport
Helsinki-Vantaa Airport
International Terminal
Tel: 818 3600
www.scandic-hotels.com/gateway
The most convenient hotel for travellers as it is actually inside the terminal. The Scandic Gateway is a small hotel with rooms in two classes – Cabin and Standard – but all are very well insulated against aircraft noise. This includes a lack of windows, but in compensation the decor of bright colours gives a feeling of spaciousness. €€€

Hotel Linna
Lönnrotinkatu 29
Tel: 020 3444 100
Fax: 010 3444 101
www.palacekamp.fi
Dating from 1903, the Lord Hotel has the most unusual façade of any hotel in Helsinki, of rustic stone with a central circular tower. Near the centre, it has 48 rooms and two suites. There's a good restaurant, a cellar bar, two saunas and Jacuzzi, plus a VIP sauna and sauna lounge. €€–€€€

Helka Hotel
Pohjoinen Rautatiekatu 23
Tel: 800 169 069
Fax: 441 087
www.helka.fi
A medium-sized independent hotel, within easy walking distance of the Central Railway Station, the Helka has 150 rooms, of which three are suites and two are for people with disabilities, There's also a restaurant, a café and a sauna. €€

Hostal Erottajanpuisto
Uudenmaankatu 9
Tel: 642 169
Fax: 680 2757
www.erottajanpuisto.com
Right in the centre, this hotel has just 15 rooms, from singles to those accommodating up to seven people. It's on the third floor (with no lift), and the toilet and shower facilities are in the hallway. €€

Hotel Arthur
Vuorikatu 19
Tel: 173 441
Fax: 626 880
www.hotelarthur.fi
This attractive, central hotel has an international ambience and extensive conference facilities. There are 144 rooms, including several family rooms and two suites. There's a restaurant, a bar, a summer terrace and two family saunas. €€

Hotel Aurora
Helsinginkatu 50
Tel: 770 100
Fax: 770 10200
www.hotelaurorahelsinki.com
About 2km (1 mile) outside the centre, in the Olympic Stadium area, this hotel has 70 rooms, a brasserie, an à la carte restaurant, two saunas, a pool and gym. €€

Hotel Anton
Paasivuorenkatu 1
Tel: 774 900
Fax: 701 4527
www.hotelanton.fi
This is a private, non-smoking hotel located just outside the city centre. It has 32 rooms – some of which don't have en-suite shower and toilet – and offers a full breakfast. €€

Eurohostel Oy
Linnankatu 9
Tel: 622 0470
Fax: 655 044
www.eurohostel.fi
Some 2km (1 mile) from the centre, this hotel has 135 rooms, including 10 triples, all with shared showers and toilets. There's a restaurant, too – the Katajanmarja. €

HEALTH AND EMERGENCIES

Medical Services
Travellers from the UK, the Republic of Ireland and other EU member countries, will be liable for the same charges as Finnish residents for urgent medical care during a temporary stay. A passport and E111 form are proof of entitlement for travellers from the

UK and the Republic of Ireland. Despite this, private travel insurance is a good idea. Visitors from other countries are specifically advised to purchase travel insurance before leaving home.

Emergencies

The all-purpose emergency number for police, fire, ambulance and rescue services is **112**, and is free from public phone boxes. There's also a 24-hour medical advice hotline: tel: 10 023.

Mehiläinen, tel: 010 414 4266, www.mehilainen.fi, is a private medical care organisation that will send a doctor to your hotel. There is also a 24-hour emergency duty clinic, tel: 010 414 0444; and the Airport Medical Centre, tel: 010 414 2702, which functions Monday to Friday 8am–8pm.

Dental Services

Contact the 24-hour medical advice hotline, tel: 10 023, and they will give details of the nearest dental surgery.

Pharmacies

Medicines are sold at pharmacies *(apteekki)* – note that chemists *(kemikaalio)* only sell cosmetics. In Helsinki Yliopiston Apteekki, Mannerheimintie 96, tel: 4178 0300, offers a 24-hour service, and others in the city centre are open until midnight.

Smoking

Smoking is not permitted within buildings that are open to the public, on public transport – although trains have smoking carriages – in schools and other educational facilities, in offices and other places of work, in areas for customers within businesses, or at public events, etc. Hotels, bars, clubs and restaurants can offer smokers' rooms. You have to be 18 years of age or more to buy cigarettes, tobacco or any other smoking products.

Crime

For the most part crime is not a serious issue in Finland. However, it is always better to be safe than sorry, so be sure to lock all valuables in the safe at your hotel, take care of your possessions in crowded places and be alert when using cash machines.

Police

The police in Finland generally keep a low profile. If you should require assistance from them, you'll find the central police station in Helsinki at Pieni Roobertinkatu 1–3, tel: 1891.

POST, COMMUNICATIONS AND NEWS

Postal Services

Stamps are available at post offices, bookshops and newsagents, and in stations and hotels. Postal rates to all countries are 65 cents for postcards and letters weighing under 20g. Poste Restante is available at the Helsinki main post office, Mannerheimintie 11F, Monday to Friday 7am–9pm, Saturday and Sunday 10am–6pm.

Telephone

The dialling code for Finland from the UK is 00 358 and from the USA and Canada 011 358. The following telephone codes should be prefixed with 0 when dialling from within Finland:

Helsinki 9
Porvoo 19
Tampere 3
Turku 2

To call Tallinn, Estonia, dial the country code (372) and then the telephone number.

Right: internet cafés are numerous

Newspapers

The best-selling papers are the Finnish *Helsingin Sanomat* and *Hufvudstadsbladet*, in Swedish. The total circulation for all newspapers is 3.3 million, which makes Finland, in terms of circulation related to population, first in Europe and third in the world. Most papers are purchased on a subscription basis rather than at shops or newsstands.

English-language newspapers, often one day late, can be found in Central Railway Station, the airport and a few other places.

Television and Radio

YLE is Finland's national public service broadcasting company. It operates five national television channels and is the only broadcaster to offer full nationwide radio coverage – in Finnish, Swedish and Sami. English-language TV, and sometimes radio, is offered in most hotels through one of the various satellite TV packages available.

LANGUAGE

The official languages of Finland are Finnish and Swedish – with about 6 percent of the population speaking the latter. Another indigenous language is Sami, spoken by the Sami people, who are better known as Lapps. Finnish, Estonian and Hungarian belong to the Finn-Ugric linguistic family. It is a language that is not understood easily by Finland's Scandinavian neighbours, let alone by English-speaking people, and it is difficult to relate the written word to the spoken language; in fact, many foreigners find it almost impossible to pronounce. However, most people speak almost perfect English, so you will have no language problems.

It is helpful to be able to recognise the Finnish words for the numbers and days:

Numbers: 0 *noll*, 1 *yksi*, 2 *kaksi*, 3 *kolme*, 4 *neljä*, 5 *viisi*, 6 *kuusi*, 7 *seitsemän*, 8 *kahdeksan*, 9 *yhdeksän*, 10 *kymmenen*, 11 *yksitoista*, 12 *kaksitoista*, 13 *kolmetoista*, 14 *neljätoista*, 15 *viisitoista*, 16 *kuusitoista*, 17 *seitsemäntoista*, 18 *kahdeksantoista*, 19 *yhdeksäntoista*, 20 *kaksikymmentä*, 30 *kolmekymmentä*, 40 *neljäkymmentä*, 50 *viisikymmentä*, 60 *kuusikymmentä*, 70 *seitsemänkymmentä*, 80 *kahdeksankymmentä*, 90 *yhdeksänkymmentä*, 100 *sata*, 200 *kaksisataa*, 1,000 *tuhat*.

Days: Monday *Maanantai*, Tuesday *Tiistai*, Wednesday *Keskiviikko*, Thursday *Torstai*, Friday *Perjantai*, Saturday *Launantai*, Sunday *Sunnuntai*.

USEFUL INFORMATION

Alcohol

The retail sale of alcoholic beverages – with the exception of medium-strength beer that can be purchased in supermarkets and other stores – is a state monopoly run along the same lines as in the other Nordic countries, excepting Denmark. The State Alcohol Company stores (Alko) are open in larger towns Monday to Friday 9am–8pm and Saturday 9am–6pm. Anyone aged 20 and over can buy any kind of alcoholic beverage at an Alko store, and those between 18 and 20 can buy mildly alcoholic beverages – at most 22 percent alcohol by volume.

Lost Property

The **Lost Property Service** (Löytötavarapalvelu) is at Kauppiaankatu 8–10, tel: 600 41006 (special rates apply); Monday to Friday 9am–6pm.

Toilets

There are automated public toilets throughout Helsinki which cost 40 cents to use. Other public toilets are located on Sofiankatu and are open May to August Monday to Friday 8am–6pm, Saturday 8am–3pm; September to April Monday to Friday 8am–2.30pm.

Above: enjoying a family day out

Travellers with Disabilities

Information and a brochure, in English and German, can be obtained from Rullaten ry, Hile Meckelborg, Pajutie 7, 02770 Espoo, Finland, tel: 805 7393, fax: 855 2470, e-mail: hile.meckelborg@rullaten.fi; www.rullaten.fi.

The City Planning Department, Helsinki Disability Board and disability organisations have put together the guide book *Accessible Helsinki*, www.hel.fi/esteeton, which can be ordered from the above address.

Children

There aren't too many places that will appeal to children here, besides the Linnanmäki Amusement Park, the Sea Life Aquarium, the Seuasaari Open-Air Museum and boat rides around the harbour.

Maps

Free city maps are available at tourist offices, in hotel lobbies and various other places.

USEFUL ADDRESSES

Tourist Offices

Helsinki City Tourist & Convention Bureau is at Pohjoisesplanadi 19, tel: 169 3757, fax: 169 3839, e-mail: tourist.info@ hel.fi, www.hel.fi/tourism. It is open May–Sept Mon–Fri 9am–8pm, Sat–Sun 9am–6pm; Oct–Apr: Mon–Fri 9am–6pm, Sat–Sun 10am–4pm.

There's a smaller tourist office at Central Railway Station's hotel booking office. Between June and August Helsinki Helpers (guides) patrol the city centre.

Porvoo City Tourist Office is at Rihkamakatu 4, tel: 520 2316, fax: 520 2317, e-mail: tourist.office@porvoo.fi, www. porvoo.fi. The office is open early Jun–Aug: Mon–Fri 9am–6pm, Sat–Sun 10am–4pm; Sept–May Mon–Fri 9.30am–4.30pm, Sat–Sun 10am–2pm.

Tampere Tourist Office is at Verkatehtaankatu 2, tel: 3146 6800, fax: 3146 6463; e-mail: touristbureau@tampere.fi, www. tampere.fi. It is open Jun–Aug Mon–Fri 8.30am–8pm, Sat–Sun 10am–5pm; Sept–May Mon–Fri 9am–4pm.

Turku Tourist Office is at Auragatan 4, tel: 262 7444, fax: 262 7674, e-mail: turku.

touring@tirku.fi, www.turkutouring.fi. It is open Apr–Sept Mon–Fri 8.30am–6pm, Sat–Sun 9am–4pm; Oct–Mar 10am to 3pm.

Tallinn Tourist Information Centre is at Niguliste 2/Kullassepa 4, tel: 645 777, www.tourism.tallinn.ee.

Finnish Tourist Board Offices Abroad

United Kingdom and Republic of Ireland
PO Box 33213, London W6 8JX; tel: 44 (0)20 7365 2512 (for UK); 353 (0)1 407 3362 (Republic of Ireland); fax: 44 (0)20 8600 5681, e-mail: finlandinfo.lon@mek.fi.

North America
655 Third Avenue, New York, NY 10017, tel: 1 800 FIN-INFO, fax: 1 212 885 9710, e-mail: mek.usa@mek.fi.

Embassies and Consulates

Canada: Pohjoisesplanadi 25, tel: 228 530.
Ireland: Reottajankatu 7A, tel: 646 006.
South Africa: Rahapajankatu 1 A 5, tel: 6860 3100.
UK: Itäinen Puistotie 17, tel: 2286 5100.
USA: Itäinen Puistotie 14 A, tel: 616 250.

FURTHER READING

Insight Guide Finland, Apa Publications 2003. Incisive background essays, a comprehensive guide to the country's attractions and a detailed listings section, plus full-colour maps and photographs.

A Brief History of Finland, Matti Klinge. General well-written history.

Sveaborg Suomenlinna, C J Gardberg and K Palsila.

Food from Finland, Anna-Maija and Juha Tanttu. Thoughtful cookery book with recipes and lots of interesting background info.

Helsinki: an Architectural Guide.

Finnish Art over the Centuries, Markku Valkonen. Concise and richly illustrated.

The Kalevala, translated by Keith Bosley, Oxford University Press. Classic edition of Elias Lönnrot's national epic, which is based on folk poems of Finland and Karelia.

practical information

ART & PHOTO CREDITS

All photography by	**Gregory Wrona** *except*
65, 67	**Mockford/Bonetti**
10	**Lyle Lawson**
12, 14	**Bettmann/Corbis**
11, 13	**Stapleton Collection/Corbis**
15	**Hulton-Deutsch Collection/Corbis**
16	**Chris Lisle/Corbis**
Front Cover	**Getty**
Back Cover	**Gregory Wrona**
Map Production	**Mapping Ideas Ltd**
Cartographic Assistance	**Tuukka Asplund & Mari Mikkola**

Cartography	**Zöe Goodwin**
Cover Design	**Klaus Geisler**

INDEX